Feng Shui for Beginners

A Complete Guide to Using Feng Shui to Achieve Balance, Harmony, Health and Prosperity in Your Home and Life!

Carol Tiebert

3rd Edition

Feng Shui for Beginners: A Complete Guide to Using Feng Shui to Achieve Balance, Harmony, Health and Prosperity in Your Home and Life! – 3rd Edition

Feng Shui for Beginners: A Complete Guide to Using Feng Shui to Achieve Balance, Harmony, Health and Prosperity in Your Home and Life! – 3ʳᵈ Edition

TABLE OF CONTENTS

Feng Shui for Beginners: A Complete Guide to Using Feng Shui to Achieve Balance, Harmony, Health and Prosperity in Your Home and Life! – 3rd Edition

Feng Shui for Beginners: A Complete Guide to Using Feng Shui to Achieve Balance, Harmony, Health and Prosperity in Your Home and Life! – 3rd Edition

Feng Shui for Beginners: A Complete Guide to Using Feng Shui to Achieve Balance, Harmony, Health and Prosperity in Your Home and Life! – 3rd Edition

Feng Shui for Beginners: A Complete Guide to Using Feng Shui to Achieve Balance, Harmony, Health and Prosperity in Your Home and Life! – 3rd Edition

Introduction

I want to thank you and congratulate you for purchasing the book, *"Feng Shui for Beginners: A complete guide to using Feng Shui to achieve balance, harmony, health and prosperity in your home and life!"*

This book contains proven steps and strategies on how to use the powers of Feng Shui to attract balance, harmony, health and prosperity within your home life.

Life on this planet can become hectic and complicated. It can be chaotic and full of negativity. Problems can arise. Relationships can be shattered. Unbeknown to a lot of people, Feng Shui can help them attract the positive energies to keep their home balanced and harmonized so that they can enjoy healthier and more prosperous lives.

This book will provide some simple suggestions that can help everyone attract positive energies. By following these simple steps, the readers will surely notice that their lives are less stressful and chaotic. They'll feel that they've become healthier and more prosperous.

You will learn the different ways in which you can overcome the loss of positive energy. In the first chapter, you will come across different aspects of Feng Shui. It is after this that you will learn about the different theories and principles that of Feng Shui. These principles are essential to learn since they are interrelated and are essential to know. You learn about the Bagua theory, which is the most prominent theory in modern Feng Shui. It is based on the different theories that have been mentioned earlier.

You have then come to understand the different steps that you will need to undertake when you are working on organizing your house through Feng Shui. You will have to first work on decluttering your house. What is decluttering? Before you come to that question you have to think about what clutter is. Only when you understand that will you be able to understand what decluttering is. You have been given a seven-step method that you can follow to ensure that you finish decluttering your house.

The next chapter deals with the different ideas of Feng Shui that you can use in the different rooms in your house. It is always good to follow these steps to have a good flow of energy throughout your house. There is another chapter that deals with the different types of décor that you must own to make sure that your house is appealing.

Thanks again for buying this book and I hope that the information contained in it will make your life more rewarding.

Chapter 1: What Is Feng Shui?

In Chinese philosophy, Feng Shui is a system of harmonizing the surrounding environment with the people. Translated into English, it means, "wind-water." As one of the Arts of Chinese Metaphysics, Feng Shui is a physiognomy. So, it's mainly about observing appearances through calculations and formulas. The practice deals with architecture in terms of invisible forces, which bind the people, Earth and the universe together. Throughout history, Feng Shui has been used to orient important structures auspiciously. A compass, stars or bodies of water often reference the site. In the 1960s, the practice of Feng Shui was suppressed in China. However, it has gained popularity since then.

The History of Feng Shui

The Hongshan and Yangshao cultures are said to be the early civilizations that practiced Feng Shui. It is believed that Feng Shui relied on astronomy before the magnetic compass was invented. Banpo houses were aligned with Yingshi for solar gain in 4000 BC. Also referred to as Ding, Yingshi was used to know the correct time to build a city during the Zhou era. In 3000 BC, the Yangshao site had a palace-like structure, which faced the south and stood on the north-south axis.

In 4000 BC, a Puyang tomb had a Chinese star map of Tiger and Dragon asterisms and a depiction of the Big Dipper. It was oriented in the north-south axis. The existence of both square and round shapes in a Longshan settlement, in the ceremonial centers in Hongshan and in the tomb in Puyang showed that gaitian cosmography existed in Chinese societies even before it emerged in the Zhou Bi Suan Jing.

Modern Feng Shui closely resembles cosmography. In 3000 BC, some formulas were seen on an unearthed jade in Hanshan. The design was linked by archaeologist, Li Xuegin, to luopan, zhinan zhen and liuren astrolabe. In Erlitou, Feng Shui was followed in the layout and design of every capital city. The Kaogong ji was responsible for these Feng Shui rules during the Zhou era. For builders, they followed the codified rules in Lu ba jing, a carpenter's manual. Feng Shui rules were also followed in the building of tombs and graves.

Instruments and Techniques Used in Early Feng Shui Practices

Present Feng Shui techniques can be traced to Neolithic China. Other techniques were just added during the Ming, Song, Tang and Han dynasties. Gnomon, an original instrument used in Feng Shui, was used to build settlements by determining the north-south axis. In Xiaotun, the Shang palaces are found 10 degrees east of north. The gnomon divided the angle between the sunset and sunrise directions to determine the north. This made the Shang walls at Zhengzhou and Yanshi align precisely. A diviner is needed in using a Feng Shui instrument to perform the rituals and determine the sky phenomena.

The liuren astrolabes include a 2-sided, lacquered board with astronomical sightlines. They are used to record the Taiyi motion through the 9 palaces. Examples of the board were unearthed during the 278 and 209 BC. The marking of a magnetic compass and the liuren astrolabes are said to be similar. Invented for Feng Shui, the magnetic compass included a south-pointing spoon or Luopan.

Feng Shui Theories

The Qi is a life force of negative or positive energies, which can be moved. It includes the interaction, age and orientation of a structure with its environment, including the soil quality, vegetation, slope of the land and the local microclimates. Structures and graves must be appropriately sited to take advantage of the qi.

The flow of qi can be determined through the luopan, a magnetic compass that reflects geomagnetism. The quality of qi can rise and fall over time because space weather also changes. Using the compass, Feng Shui can be a type of divination, which determines the local environment quality. A good qi is often associated with an individual with good karma.

In Feng Shui, the yin and yang theory is an expression of polarity. Like a magnetic dipole, the yang creates the effort and the yin receives it. There are five elements essential to life: wood, fire, metal, water and earth. These polarities cancel each other on Earth. The yin and yang forces are used in Feng Shui to align an object, site, building or city.

The Bagua is widely used in Feng Shui. The River Chart and the Luoshu were linked with the Turtle Calendar, which dates back to 2300 BC, and to the astronomical events in 6 BC. The cardinal directions of the Yaodian are known as the 4 Celestial animals: Azure Dragon, Vermilion Bird, White Tiger and Black Tortoise. During the Shang dynasty, the diagrams were also linked with the method of divination known as sifang. In Hongshan culture, the diagrams were used in astronomy. These theories have been explained in detail in the next chapter.

Traditional Feng Shui

The traditional system is based on the observation of earthly space and heavenly time. Feng Shui is actually among the oldest schools of thought. It was described in the Book of Tomb in the Han dynasty and in The Book of Burial in the Jin dynasty. It was concerned with the orientation and location of tombs. Then, it also considered buildings and homes. The form refers to the environment's shape and takes into consideration the 5 celestial animals: yellow snake, black turtle, white tiger, green dragon and the phoenix. It also considers the 5 traditional elements like water, metal, earth, fire and wood, as well as the yin-yang concept. The school analyzes the flow of the water and wind, and the shape of the land to locate a place for the ideal qi. Furthermore, it also includes the timing of important events like the birth date of the resident.

The Compass School, on the other hand, is just a recent Feng Shui technique, which is founded on the 8 cardinal directions. Each of these directions has a unique qi. It makes use of the Luopan. The Compass School was linked with numerous techniques, including the 8 Mansions and the Flying Star. Masters of traditional Feng Shui passed the techniques through books and oral teachings.

Modern Feng Shui Techniques
Modern Feng Shui is a simplified version of the traditional one. Its main focus is on the Bagua. The 8 Life Aspirations is a simple Feng Shui system, which relates each cardinal direction with a certain life aspiration like fame, wealth, family, etc.

Thomas Lin Yun introduced the Black Sect Tantric Buddhism Feng Shui in the United States in the 1970s. It is a religion, which incorporates Feng Shui, Tibetan Buddhism, Taoism and transcendentalism. It is mainly concerned with the building's interior. The Bagua is put on the entryway. Each sector of the Bagua represents a certain part in a human being's life.

Modern Uses of Traditional Feng Shui
Landscape ecologists use Feng Shui in their studies. In Asia, old existing forests are considered Feng Shui woods, related with the preservation of different fauna and flora species, historical continuity and cultural heritage. Some studies reveal that these forests indicate the environmental and sustainability components of healthy homes in ancient Feng Shui practices.

Landscape architects and environmental scientists also use traditional Feng Shui and its practices in their projects. Architects also use Feng Shui in their study of unique and ancient Asian architectural traditions. Geographers, on the other hand, analyze methods and techniques to find historical sites in Canada and in the American Southwest.

Chapter 2: The Theories And Principles Of Feng Shui

This chapter deals with the most important theories and principles. The Feng Shui for living is based on these theories! The first chapter provides you with the basic details on what the theories are. This chapter will cover them extensively. The later chapters will describe how you must use Feng Shui and its theories to ensure that you have a very good way of living. The first part of the chapter addresses the principles of Feng Shui.

Principles of Feng Shui

Feng Shui is not only about moving the furniture around in your house, but is a style of living. There are different concepts and theories that underlie the need to reposition the furniture and décor in your house or your office. For this, you will need to understand the theories that make Feng Shui what it is. There are however, certain principles that you will need to know before you get into the idea of Feng Shui.

Balance and Stability

Feng Shui is a principle that works towards maintaining a balance in your life. It also helps in having homogeneity in the different types of energies that are found within your home and office. This balance and homogeneity is achieved through the arrangement of color, décor, furniture and your association with different objects in your immediate environment. There are two theories that help you achieve a great sense of stability – the Five Earth elements theory and the Bagua theory. The Bagua is a mix of the Earth elements theory as well. It is a pattern or a design that can be followed throughout your apartment. The Feng Shui has theories that are unique to people. If the Five elements theory worked with a friend, it may not work for you. But it is always best to use the different theories together since they provide the best results.

An optimistic and positive view

When you use Feng Shui in your house, you will find yourself with a renewed sense of optimism and positivity. There are a lot of people who have begun to use Feng Shui in their homes on account of needing a certain amount of positivity at home. Through Feng Shui, you will be able to ensure that there is a good amount of positive energy. This energy will ensure that you are optimistic and energetic. You will find that you are less irritated when compared to what you used to be. You will also find that through the inflow of positive energy, the negative energy and its different forms are also eliminated from your home. If there is any bad luck that has been cast on any part of your house, you will be able to eliminate it too through the positive energy that has begun to flow into your house.

Symmetrical Beauty

Symmetrical beauty is one of the main ideas of Feng Shui. It is through this principle that Feng Shui states that every entity in the universe is beautiful. Feng Shui tries to bring out the beauty and the symmetry of the different entities that you own. There are many people who believe that Feng Shui is a practice of celebrating beauty. This is done through the aligning the different physical elements in your immediate environment.

Promoting the love for the environment

In the theories mentioned below, it is stated that Feng Shui believes that there is a universal energy, called the Chi that is found in every entity in the universe. The Theory on the five elements of the earth believes that as a person, you need to ensure that you are aware of the environment that is around you. You have to develop respect for that environment as well. You will then be able to take care of your surroundings with care. You will know if there is any form of negative energy in the vicinity and will learn how to remove that. This will help you become successful.

A picture of self – love

The different principles of Feng Shui had been devised to ensure that you begin to appreciate and love yourself. These principles ensure that you arrange the objects you own and also the house you live in in a way that will help you overcome any pessimism. You will be able to learn that the negative energy that has infested itself in you will diminish and give way to the positive energy. This energy will help you love yourself and will also help you increase your productivity. You can love yourself, but you should ensure that you do not love yourself to the point of madness. You cannot assume that you are beyond the people around you. You will have to ensure that you do not indulge in activities that are counter – productive to you.

Dreaming

The different principles that are entailed in Feng Shui are used to relate the different entities that are found in your surroundings. These entities also include the energies in your body. The different entities often form a network that has multiple layers. These layers play a key role when you dream. You will be able to ensure that the dream has been entangled in this network. Once the network has captured the dreams, you will be provided with different paths, which will help you accomplish those dreams. You will have seen that there are people who have big dreams but have an environment that does not allow them to cater to those very dreams. It is the same for you too. If you are a person who dreams big, you will also need to change the environment around you. It is only when this happens that you will be able to achieve you final goals!

Feng Shui for Beginners: A Complete Guide to Using Feng Shui to Achieve Balance, Harmony, Health and Prosperity in Your Home and Life! – 3rd Edition

Feng Shui is a different way of living! You have now gathered that it is through Feng Shui that you will be able to ensure that you have a sense of stability in your life. You will also be able to ensure that you are one step towards achieving your goals.

The Theories of Feng Shui

There are four different theories that have been used in Feng Shui. These theories are interrelated and can be used together. The first theory, which is the theory of the universal energy, is the sole basis for every other theory. It is believed that the chi is found in every entity in the universe. The other two theories mentioned in this section are the very common theories. However, the fourth theory, called Bagua, is used extensively in the modern world. This theory is covered in detail in the next chapter.

The theory of the Universal Energy, Chi

This is a theory that has been passed through generations in China. The ancient Chinese believed that every entity in the universe has an energy called the Chi, which is the universal energy. This energy exists in every object that is found in the universe. It does not matter whether or not the object is animate or inanimate. The Chi is the energy that is used as the sole basis in both the Yin and Yang theory and the Theory of the five elements.

The theories in Feng Shui believe that this energy manifests itself in every object that is found in the universe. This shows that this energy can manifest itself in colors and decors. There may be many objects in your house where you will find the Chi. The basic idea of Feng Shui is to attract the energy into the different objects in your house. When the energy is attracted by the different entities, you will find that it flows into your body. This will ensure that there is a good balance of positive energy in your body.

It is extremely important that you have a good amount of chi in the immediate environment. If this energy is found in a good amount, you will be able to ensure that this energy flows throughout your body. There are different tips that have been mentioned in the book, which will help, you ensure that the Chi flows freely through every corner in your house. When you are working on the Feng Shui at home, try to identify the flow of the Chi!

The 5 Elements of Feng Shui

Feng Shui in when translated into English means wind and water respectively. It is due to this name that the theory of the five elements had arisen in Feng Shui. The five elements that have been considered in this theory are metal, wind, water, earth and fire. When you design your workplace or your apartment, you need to ensure that there is a balance between these five elements. It is only then that you will be able to ensure that you are able to stay positive. You will also be able to mold yourself to become one of the elements depending on what you need. This can only happen when there is a certain amount of balance between the energies in these elements.

The Metal Elements

It is good to ensure that these elements are a part of your furnishing. If they are a part of the furnishing, you will be able to ensure that you have constant financial success. The different objects and colors to which this element is associated are silver, marble, stone, gold and the objects made from them. The western part of your house is the best place for your metal elements.

The Wood Elements

Wood provides a sense of support to you. You will find that these elements represent a sense of loyalty and also help in improving your creativity. These elements are available in multiple forms. You can use wooden furniture or panels and walls. You can use different shades of green apart from the color brown. If your wood element is stationary, the eastern corner of your house is preferred. The same applies for your room.

Fire Elements

The elements of fire represent your passion. They talk about your efficiency and the way you work to ensure that you get your job done. You have to ensure that you position all your fire elements towards the southern part of your house. If you are working on the elements in the room, ensure that your fire elements are facing the southern corner of the room. These elements are the strongest elements of the five mentioned in this section. You have to take care when you install a fire element in your home. Red is the color linked most to the fire elements. It is also welcoming and calm to look at. You can have a fireplace or candles and lamps at home to depict the fire elements.

Earth Elements

The elements of the earth offer you a foundation that is firm and resilient to develop the relationship that you share with the members in your family. You can have colors that represent the earth – green, brown, yellow and orange. These colors offer your family a lot of strength. You can have objects that are made from clay or mud. This will ensure that there is a semblance of stability in your home. The center of the room is the best place to position this element. You can have wooden tables and chairs since they will help in keeping your family grounded.

Water Elements

Miniature fountains or aquariums often represent the water elements. You can have a fish tank in your house since that will help in letting the connection between the members of your family, flow like the flow of the water. When there are elements of water in your house, you will be able to ensure that there is better communication within the family. You can also have colors, like blue and black, which represent water, in your house. This will ensure that there is a balance in the energies that are flowing through your house. It is always good to position this element in the northern part of your house!

The Yin and Yang theory

The Yin and Yang theory is an ancient Chinese theory that has been taught in different schools. This theory is the mother of all other theories. The different arts in China like the martial arts, the Taoism cosmology and even Feng Shui depend on the working of the Yin and Yang theory.

According to this theory, the different entities in the universe have two opposing energies – the Yin and the Yang. These forces, however, have a deep connection between them. They depict the nature of the human beings. The Yin energy represents feminine energy while the Yang energy represents the masculine energy.

The two forces interact with each other and create the essence of life. These energies are independent of each other but they depend on each other when it comes to their existence. This means that they function independently, but need each other when it comes to their existence. It is due to the fact that they are opposite to each other that make them attract towards each other.

In the Chinese tradition, the color black represents the Yin energy, while the Yang energy is represented by a soft white. Although the color black represents the Yin energy, it represents calm and softness. This energy is a very silent force. The Yin energy can be found in the universe as the beautiful mystery of the moon and the richness of the soil. It is also a representative of the softness of the water.

The Yang force is the complete opposite of the Yin force. The Yang force, although represented by white is not the calm energy. The bright colors, the racing cars and the heat of the Sun often represent it. It can also be represented by the solid nature of a rock!

The Yin and Yang energies are a contrast. The Yin energy can be compared to the mystery of the night while the Yang energy can be compared to the heat of the Sun during summer.

Feng Shui works on maintaining the balance between these energies. But before you try to work on maintaining a balance between these forces, you will have to learn the application of this theory on a very simple level. It is only when you do this that you will be able to benefit with an immense amount of positivity in your life.

Feng Shui for Beginners: A Complete Guide to Using Feng Shui to Achieve Balance, Harmony, Health and Prosperity in Your Home and Life! – 3rd Edition

The Yin Energy

The Yin energy is the passive form of energy. It is often called the feminine energy. This energy relaxes you when you need to be calm. The bathroom and the bedroom have a good amount of the Yin energy. You have to ensure that there is a good amount of Yin energy in these rooms. You will need to have soft music and portraits in these rooms.

The Yang Energy

The Yang is the energy that is vibrant and active. It is associated with strong color, lights, loud sound and music. These indicate a force that keeps rising. It is essential to ensure that the Yang energy is distributed all over your house. It has to be distributed evenly at your work place too. Make sure that you have a good amount of Yang energy at home when you host parties.

It is easy for the entities in your house to separate the Yin and the Yang energies. It is for this very reason that you will need to strike a balance between these two energies. When you have a home that has been arranged through the principles of Feng Shui, you will find that there is homogeneity in the workings of both the energies in their active and passive states. The world now is fast paced and it is due to this that you will always find an imbalance of these energies. The world is fast and feisty resulting in an excessive amount of Yang energy. It is because of this that you lose out on the Yin energy. This balance will have to be maintained.

Objects that attract the Yin Energy in Your Home

Your bedroom is the room that is full of Yin energy. However, there are imbalances that will occur in your room on account of the Yang elements that are present. You have to get rid of those items in your room soon! This process is called decluttering. You will learn how to declutter in the later chapters.

You however should not remove every entity that represents your Yang energy. The last part of this section explains to you about why this should not be done. There needs to be a balance that is maintained. You cannot have an overdose of the Yin energy in your room since that may make you lethargic. You will hence have to ensure that there is certain amounts of Yang energy in the room, which will help you, balance the Yin energy. You could have bright colored walls or objects in your room. You can also have bright colored linens!

Objects that attract the Yang Energy in Your Home

There are certain places in your house that are the hotspots for the Yang energy. According to the Feng Shui theory, the living room, family room, study table, kitchen and your office room are the hubs for the Yang energy. You will need to strike a balance with the Yin energy. You can use bright colors and upbeat music. There is a certain type of décor that you can use in these rooms to ensure that there is a flow of positive energy.

How do you balance the Yin and Yang

There are times when you will feel an imbalance at your home or at your workplace. This is most often due to an imbalance between the Yin and Yang. You may now wonder how you can remove these imbalances. It is not a very difficult process.

When you are working on balancing the Yin energy in your house, you will need to introduce objects that represent relaxing energies. For instance, they could be objects that represent the earth elements. If you need to balance the Yang energy, you will need to add objects that have bright colors. You will learn about the influence of colors on Feng Shui in the later chapters. You can use music and bright colors to help you restore the balance.

It may be difficult to attain a balance between the Yin and Yang energies. But when you do strike that balance, you will be able to ensure that you have a lot of positive energy that is flowing through your house. This balance will help you achieve prosperity and happiness.

The Bagua

The Bagua is the modern theory of Feng Shui. This theory incorporates the Five-element theory and also the theory of the universal energy. It is the theory that is used most often in these times!

The Bagua is a chart that is used to help you understand the energy in the different parts of the house. You will be able to understand the energy that is found in the different parts of the environment that is surrounding your house too. The shape of the chart was derived from the pattern that exists on the turtle's shell. The chart has nine locations on it depicting the different aspects of life.

There is energy that is found in each of these locations. This energy is affected by many factors. The energy works in a correlated manner. You will find that there needs to be a balance between these energies. When there is a balance between these energies, we will be in a state of Unity called Tai Chi. It is only when you are in this state of unity that you will be able to prosper.

When you would like to use the Bagua to rearrange your house you will have to follow certain steps.

You will first have to draw the print of your house from the top view. When you do this, you will need to use the Bagua map to view the areas of your house. The entrance or your main door must be at the bottom of the map since this is the place from where the energy leaves your house. Once you have identified the different parts of your house on the Bagua map, you can try to associate the different elements to the parts of your house. You will then have to ensure that there is a balance between the energies that exist in these elements. Only when this is done, you will be able to ensure that there is stability in your life. The next chapter provides you with a detailed description of the Bagua.

Chapter 3: The Bagua

The previous chapter gave you a little introduction on what the Bagua is. The Bagua is very important when it comes to modern Feng Shui.

The Bagua, or the Pa Kua, is a chart that is used by most people to understand and anticipate the power of the energy in the different parts of their surroundings and in their life. The shape of a turtle's shell depicts the Bagua chart. This chart provides you with a layout consisting of nine locations. These locations are associated with the different aspects of your life.

There is energy that is contained in these locations too! This energy is affected by many external factors. The layout has been separated into eight different sectors. These sectors have to work in relation with each other. It is only when the energy in these eight sectors is balanced that you will experience a sense of harmony. You will be able to see that the energy that is in your house is unified. When you achieve this state of unity, you will be able to experience the state of ultimate health. This is the state that every person has always strived to achieve.

For you to understand the eight factors better, let us deal with certain examples dealing with each chapter.

Fire
Fire is the most important factor in your life. It is to do with the enlightenment and the fame that you will receive and achieve. It also deals with illumination. Through this sector, you will be able to identify if there is something that is missing in your life. You will also have to identify if you have fulfilled your dreams.

Through this sector, you will be able to identify the questions that you have in life. You will also be able to identify whether the answers come from you, or whether you seek them from the outside. Through this element, you will be able to grow closer to your very essence. You will be able to reach the brightness that is inside you and pull it out.

Water
Water is the most soothing sector. This element directly affects your life's path and the career that you have chosen. You will be able to identify how you feel about all the work that you do. You will be able to identify if there is something more that you are looking for with respect to your career.

Feng Shui for Beginners: A Complete Guide to Using Feng Shui to Achieve Balance, Harmony, Health and Prosperity in Your Home and Life! – 3rd Edition

There may be many questions that you have about your life. You will be able to answer them with ease. You will know whether or not you are comfortable with continuing on the path that you have chosen. You will know whether you are walking into a path that is full of obstacles. You will be able to gather whether or not you are affected by the flow of life.

Earth

This element is what keeps you grounded. You will be able to know more about all your relationships, about love and about marriage in general. You do not have to be with a person to have a relationship. You have a relationship with the people around you. You could either be single or married but you do have a social relationship. Through this element, you will be able to gather whether or not you are engaged in a healthy relationship.

There are times when you may be craving for a relationship. You may be unhappy about where you stand in a relationship. It is at these times that the element helps washing peace all over you. You will be able to identify if you have a good relationship with your co – workers and your friends and family. You will be able to decipher the depths of your relationships.

Mountain

The mountain sector deals with the way you perceive situations and the way you perceive the higher power. It provides you with wisdom and self – improvement. In most of the Chinese texts, it is said that your inner stillness is your mountain. It is what helps you stay strong.

The mountain within you helps you understand what spiritual life is to you. You will be able to attain a sense of calm when you meditate. This is because of the fact that you will feel the silence that is found in the mountains. You will be able to answer certain questions that always haunt you. You will try to understand whether or not spirituality is a part of you and your life. You will also be able to see whether you are the kind of person who devotes himself to prayer at a particular time of the day.

The Lake

This is what describes your creativity. You will be able to gather a good amount of knowledge about your offspring and the projects that you may take up in the future. This sector is very important when it comes to understanding the relationship that you share with your children. This relationship could be with respect to your children or the children around you.

The other aspect that you learn from this sector is whether or not you are creative when it comes to your projects. The relationship that you share and your creativity both come from your inner spirit. You will find yourself answering many questions when you are around this sector. The first is whether or not you are able to work fully and well on all your projects. You will know if you have an obstacle when it comes to your creativity. If you often find yourself around children, you will know whether or not you are kind to them. If you are not kind then you will learn why that is the case.

Thunder

Thunder is another important element in the Bagua. You will have to ensure that you have the best décor and arrangement of that décor in the area. This element helps you identify the relationship that you share with your community and the people in it. It moreover helps you identify the relationship that you share with your elders or your ancestors.

You will be able to answer the following questions.

1. Do you have a good relationship with your teachers and your mentors?
2. Do you have loving memories of your parents?
3. Do you have a loving relationship with your family?
4. How do you feel when you find yourself not appreciated by your family?

Heaven

This sector does not deal with God or your spirituality. It deals with the way your friends are with you. It deals with your levels of compassion. You will know if you have a group of friends or colleagues who are genuine. You will be able to identify whether or not they are worth your time and your money. You will be able to understand if you can rely on them when you are in need or generally.

You will know whether you or your friends have the compassion to deal with voluntary activities. If there are selfless people around you, you will be able to identify them. You will also be able to tell if they are the ones you can count on. You have to know if there are people around you whom you can always lean on or the people who will help you without you having to ask them. Remember that it has to be both ways.

The Wind

It is said that the wind carries all your energy. This wind is what deals with your fortunate blessings. It is always with respect to your prosperity. You will be able to know how wealthy you will be and will also understand whether you will attain financial abundance.

You will find yourself free from the constant worry that you have about money and wealth. If you are in debt, there will be a way out, something that was staring you in the face for so long. You will also be able to ensure that you have a good flow of money into your bank account. If there is a good amount of energy in this area, you will find yourself with a good amount of money with you. You will have a lot of blessings from the material world.

The Tai Chi

This energy, also called the Qi or the Universal Energy is the most important aspect of Feng Shui. In the previous chapter, you learnt about what the Chi is and how it works in Feng Shui. In the Bagua theory, it is said that this energy is what contains all the other energies. When this energy is balanced, you will have good health and unity!

How to strike a balance between the energies

In the previous section, you learnt about the essence of the energies in the eight sectors of the Bagua. It was said there needs to be a balance that exists between these energies. This section will tell you which sector has to be paired with which sector in order to strike a balance.

You will need to ensure that you strike a balance between the following:

1. Fire and Water.
2. Lake and Mountain.
3. Wind and Thunder.
4. Heaven and Earth.

Now let us try to understand why you need to strike a balance between the energy that is found in these sectors?

Let us talk about the first pair. You would have achieved fame through illumination because of the energy that is found in the Fire sector. But how long do you think this can go on for? You need the fame and the prominence to flow like the water. It should never dry up.

The lake is what helps you understand your creativity. Let us assume that you have constructed a new house. You have decided to paint it bright colors and have art done on the walls. You are trying to be creative. But there is one problem here. You cannot expect to have a very colorful house. It does not bode well with the eyes! This is where the mountain comes in. You will be able contemplate on whether the decisions you have made are good for you or not.

The wind and the thunder are very closely related. The wind deals with your blessings and the thunder relates with your relationships with your elders. You will be able to balance out the blessings that you receive from your elders if you balance these two energies.

The final pair is of great importance! You will have to know whether you share a good relationship with your friends or not. To ensure that the relationship is good, you will have to make sure that you have the correct balance between these two energies.

It is always a good thing to understand the relationship between the different sectors. It is also good to know how they are interrelated. You will have to see how you can balance these energies to ensure that you attain the perfect balance, the Tai Chi. It is true that only when you have good relationships, you will have good blessings. You need to ensure that you have great relationships with your friends and your ancestors in order to be fortunate in life. You will need to contemplate and meditate well in order to reach higher levels of creativity. You will also be able to identify your capability and potential when you meditate. When you realize your potential and act up on it, you will be able to obtain the material benefits like wealth and prosperity. When you are a true and a good friend, you will be able to obtain a positive energy. When you strike this balance, you will be at peace.

Chapter 4: How Do You Use Bagua In Your Buildings And Houses?

You have been told all you need to know about the Bagua. But how will you use it on your house? This chapter gives you the details on how to use the Bagua on your house.

You will have to first draw the layout of your house. You have to have the blueprint or your architect's drawings to your house. You will need to have the perfect view of the building. You will have to look at it from the top. This is the only way you will be able to identify the rooms in your house.

Every home or a building is a manmade structure. These structures are measured on squares alone. The Bagua for the house also is based on a square. The wind, fire and the earth elements occupy the top of the square. The Thunder, the Tai Chi and the lake occupy the middle of the square while the mountain, water and heaven lie at the base of the square. The front door or the entrance to any room must be at the base of the square. This is the Bagua structure that you will have to follow for every room in your house! If your room is in the shape of a rectangle, you could stretch the Bagua to fit.

If there are parts that you will have to extend or if there are certain parts in the blueprint you could either look for a way to compensate or you could use a shape that you think fits the missing part of your house. This shape could be made on any scale. It does not have to be one scale in particular.

Once you have identified the Bagua to your room or your house, you will want to make changes. Make sure that these changes are gradual. You could start off with a table or a chair in the rooms. Once you are comfortable with these changes, you could move to the bigger changes. You will just have to ensure that the changes you are making conform to the Bagua.

When you are working on remodeling your house, you will have to ensure that the Bagua map is positioned in a way that you have your main entrance or the front door at the bottom of the map. When you do build a house, you generally make sure that the front door is in the Mountain, Water or the Heaven sectors. But there are times when your door may be in a deep alcove. There are times when you have multiple entrances to a room. In such situation, you will have to use the main entrance. For instance, consider two rooms with adjoining bathrooms. There are two entrances to the bedrooms. But the main entrance is the one that leads you into the corridor or the living room in your house. You should remember that every section of the Bagua that is corresponds to the part of your room has the energy that is found in the Bagua map! This energy governs your life!

This is a type of arrangement or Feng Shui that has lasted for over 4,000 years! This has often been called Black Hat Feng Shui. Although it is old, it has been used in the West in the recent times. The Chinese had a Bagua compass that they used to place the different sectors in the room. This compass is held in the upside down position. If you think carefully about it, you will realize that the North of your room should be at the bottom of the room or at the bottom of the Bagua square. This has a very different meaning to all the areas in the room and the energies that they contain. It is very different when your main door is on the North side of your room.

In Traditional Chinese Feng Shui, it has been seen that the Black hat method is rarely considered. The main aspects that are considered are the details about the occupants of the house and the type of furniture that is used. It takes a very long time to understand these details.

The initial idea of Feng Shui was to identify the electromagnetic fields and the electromagnetic energy of the earth and see how it affects the energy that is found in the universe. It is difficult to use those as the basis because of the increased usage of electronic gadgets. These electronic gadgets have a strong electromagnetic field. This field may affect the electromagnetic field of the earth. There is a possibility that the effect of the electromagnetic field of the earth washes out!

For a beginner, it is always good to ensure that you use the main or entrance door method. This is the easiest way since you this relationship between the front door and the energy is always consistent and you do not need a compass to do this. The best way to see if this method works is to see how the changes affect your life.

You could do this through the following example. You should identify the one area of your life where the things are going perfectly well for you. Once you have identified that, you will need to pick the room that corresponds to that emotion. Take all the junk that you have in your house and throw it into that room. You may find that your life has suddenly taken a turn for the worse in the area you were flourishing in. There is a chance that it may take you a complete moon cycle to identify the changes. But, this does not always happen.

There may be times when a part of your room or a part of your building is missing. At such a time, the Bagua energy is low in those rooms! You could use light to fill the space up. This light could be internal or external. Let us assume that there is no room above the garage. This shows an empty spot. You could have a spotlight in your garden, which would highlight the space above the garage. This helps in energizing that area with equal amounts of energy. There are times when it is extremely difficult to illuminate an area, which has negative energy. But you could use any shiny or sparkly objects to illuminate the place. You could always create an illusion by using mirrors.

There may be times when there is a room that stands out as a projection. You could have a balcony that is projecting out! This is an extension to the Bagua Square. The energy that is contained in this area will be high! It is a very bad idea to have a projection in the Mountain region. The other sectors only make sure that they have a level of dominance over the other areas of the house.

You are always asked to be cautious when you are designing your house or any building in an unusual shape. This is due to the fact that there could be rooms or projections that could create a negative energy. You will not always be able to compensate for these negative energies. You have to ensure that you never miss out on the male Yang or the female Yin of the house. You will find that the person with the associated gender will find it very difficult to live in this place. Where either Heaven or Earth or their complementary pairs, Wind and Mountain are projections, there will be exaggerated energies of yang or yin, respectively.

The Intuitive Aspects

When you change the environment you live in you are also changing your perception of the environment. You are not trying to do this consciously, but it does happen. There are seven things or objects that can alter the energy surrounding you. They also help in adding a certain flavor to the different objects or the décor that you have at home.

1. Sight
2. Color
3. Water
4. Movement
5. Living Energy
6. Sound
7. Weight

It is true that your sight is the most important sense that you need to have in order to appreciate the environment that you are in. You will need to ensure that the environment you are in is appealing to you. But, the other senses are important too! If you listen to splashing sounds of the fountain or smell the lovely flowers blooming in the garden, you find yourself feeling positive about life. This provides you with a life affirmation.

You have heard the phrase 'Don't judge a book by its cover'. This says that you should never go by the appearance. But the truth is that the first impression that you have about a certain thing accounts for close to 50% of how you will experience that particular thing. This could be a place or an object in your home. You may have the best couches in your house, but they will never be noticed if terrible sheets have covered them.

It is always a good thing to enter your environment and try to walk through it the way you did the first time! If you find this hard, you could bring a friend over and ask him to write down how he felt about the place. You could ask them to tell you what they noticed the first time they walked into your house. When they have walked through your house, was there anything they thought that you would need to get fixed? If they found that something smelt really bad, did they try to find out why?

You have to ensure that you never deviate from your style. If you find that you love having beanbags in your living room, go ahead and do that! You should never change how you like having your house because you are applying Feng Shui. You do not have to change to the Asian décor. You could use all the guidelines that have been mentioned in order to style your environment using the objects that you have! It is always good to use your creativity in order to decorate your environment.

Chapter 5: Starting The Feng Shui Process

Feng Shui is a practice that has been followed in China since the ancient times. This method helps in bridging the gap between you and your immediate environment. This is done through a mutual benefiting relationship. This practice believes that the nature is an active source of energy. To ensure that you follow Feng Shui, you will need to work on arranging the objects you own in your house and in your workplace. This is done in a very symmetrical fashion. This symmetry helps in attracting the positive energy.

Feng Shui does not work on using expensive tools and objects to ensure that you have a home filled with a balanced amount of energy. This practice is all about trying to understand the different aspects that go into attracting the right energy towards you.

The Basics of Feng Shui for your house
It is not complicated or difficult to embrace the different ideas of Feng Shui you're your house. You can use different methods to try and ensure that you are using the different principles and theories of Feng Shui when trying to absorb the positive energy. There are certain practices that have been used to ensure that the universal energy, the chi, is found abundantly at your house! If you integrate these principles, you will never have to worry about any negativity. This section covers the basic ideas of Feng Shui.

Feng Shui, Light, Air
The windows to your apartment are your best friends. When you are constructing your house, try to ensure that you have a good number of small windows or large windows to attract the positive energy. When you want positive energy to flow through your house, you will need to ensure that there is a good amount of lighting too! The theory of Feng Shui believes that the chi flows into your house as easily as the autumn wind or the light. You will hence have to regulate the light and wind at all times to ensure that there is a good flow of the energy. When you open windows and allow all the light and wind to enter your home, you are allowing yourself to have a good amount of recycling of energies. If you live in an area where there is very bad wind, you can add an air purifier. This will ensure that there are no toxins in the air. Try to have a lot of wind enter your home. Make sure that there is a good amount of light too! If there is no light, your house will be dull which will bring you down further.

Decluttering
Decluttering is the first step towards Feng Shui. You will learn about decluttering and also the way you must declutter in the next chapters. The clutter you have at home

always forms an obstruction towards the flow of energy. This directly impacts the health of the members in your family.

Layout

When you are working on Feng Shui, you will have to work with a blueprint of your house. Try to ensure that you know every nook and corner of your house. You will be able to ensure that you have structured your house in a way that will help you ensure that there is a good flow of energy in the house.

Work on the door

You have to ensure that the front and back door to your house are not on a straight line. If they are in a straight line, you will find that the energy flows through your house without benefitting you in any manner. You should create an obstruction in such cases. You need to ensure that the energy is flowing through the house and is staying in the house for a certain amount of time.

Let there be light

You would have heard the phrase that when god said there needed to be light, there was light! That is how it should be at your home too! It is always good to have more natural light in your house; the more the light, the better the flow of the energy. You can use green plants and other green colored items since they represent the earth elements.

Water elements

These elements as mentioned above help in refreshing the energy, especially the Chi found in your home. When you have small fountains at home, you will be able to bring about a change in the fortune of your family. It is always good to position the fountain in the center of your apartment since that way you will be able to ensure that the energy is refreshed in every nook and corner of your home. If you cannot have a fountain, you can add a fish tank. Have goldfish in these tanks since they indicate a wealth! You will have to take care of the fish though and ensure that the tank is cleaned on a regular basis.

The element of Red

Red is a color that represents passion and celebration. It is a color that is appealing visually too! It is best to use this color in your bedroom and your living room. This is because of the fact that these are the rooms where you will be able to ensure that your relationships are healthy. But if there is too much of red, you may have anger issues and may also become very restless. You can use red to detail the accessories that you will be placing in your house.

The South points

When you begin marking the north points of your house, you will have to pay more attention to the south. You will have to ensure that the area is free from clutter. The south points of your house help in building relationships that are mutually satisfying. You should have objects that have pairs in this area – dolls that have been paired together.

The dining room

The dining area needs to have circular items alone since this is where you attract heavenly blessings. When you say your prayers before you eat, you are calling the divine energy which will never flow in places with sharp objects. The even number represents balance. When you have chairs at the dining table ensure that there is an even number. You do not need to have heavy decorations in your dining room. It is best to have decorations that represent health.

Exposed beams

You will have to ensure that there are no beams that have been exposed anywhere around your house. These beams create an opposition. You will find that there is no flow of energy in the house because of these obstructions. The energy then flows into the bottom, which has a negative effect on your health and your fortune.

Bedroom

Your bedroom is the place that you would want to get into when you have the urge to relax. You have to ensure that there is no mirror that is opposite your bed. This mirror brings bad luck to all your relationships.

You will be able to achieve a sense of peace at home if you find yourself decorating your house and changing it from what it used to be. You will find yourself prospering and will be able to ensure that you are healthy and wealthy. It is always good if you begin with the basics of Feng Shui before you jump into the processes that follow Feng Shui. The next chapter deals with how you must declutter before you begin to arrange your house!

Chapter 6: Feng Shui For A Balanced Home And Life

In some cases, an individual may feel that he doesn't feel good in a room but he doesn't know what's wrong. This may mean that the yin-yang isn't balanced. If he'd learn simple ways to arrange a room in his home to support the needs and activities of everyone in the house, he would be capable of creating a better sense of balance, comfort and harmony. Founded on the ancient practice of Feng Shui, the yin and yang recognize that the universe has different energy forces, which exist interdependently. These forces are like the poles of a magnet, finely balanced and attracted to each other.

The symbol of yin and yang shows a pair of fish gliding together in perfect balance. Each has a component of the other. The white fish has a black eye while the black fish has a white eye. Both fish swim together in a circle to create perfect harmony. In Feng Shui, humans are ancient creatures who seek natural balance. If the living environment is imbalanced, the human lives within that space also feel imbalanced. Therefore, each individual must learn to work with the yin and yang in their homes to create living spaces, which are supportive of the balance of life.

The yin represents qualities attributable to the female, which are yielding, dark and passive. On the other hand, the yang qualities are attributable to the male, which are extroverted, active and bright. To apply the concepts of the yin and the yang, it's a must to first identify whether the room is used as a restful or active space. Then, art, furniture, colors, shapes and objects can be incorporated to support either the restfulness or activeness of the room. If the room is for rest, the yin features are highlighted. If it is for activity, the yang features are enhanced. It is important for each room to have both features.

How to Create a Restful Space
A room can be made a restful space by incorporating yin properties. A yin room is a place where a person can calm down to support rejuvenation, relaxation and rest. It can be the dining room, bathroom, family room, living room or bedroom. Circular objects can be added to the room along with muted and darker colors. Upholstered furniture, which is more cushiony, darker and lower, can also be used. Fabrics in corduroy, velvet and chenille can be added as well. If carpet and an area rug will be used, floral or circular patterns must be used. Paint must be in softer colors and lightning must be muted.

Stucco, brick and adobe are considered yin materials. Baroque, as well as the eras of Louis IV, Louis V and Victoria, is considered in design history as a period wherein yin qualities were incorporated in the home. If the room has a lot of yin properties, detailed patterns must be removed. Furniture and art must have modern and straighter lines. Pillows and area rugs must also be removed. Smaller things and plants can also be taken out. The room can be Zen-like so that it can breathe. Paints can be in brighter or pastel colors. Tiles or hardwood can be used instead of carpets. Curtains must be removed and light-colored shutters must be used to open up the room.

How to Create an Active Space

An active room can be a study room, hallway, laundry room, garage, playroom, workout room, home office or kitchen. If a person wants a more active room, he can include accessories, which have straighter lines and less detail, un-upholstered furniture that is square-shaped or has more angles, bolder colors and/or whites and brighter lightning. Large prints in geometrical shapes and bold stripes can bring out the yang qualities together with synthetics, silks, vinyl, plastics and leather. In terms of construction materials, tiles, cement, hardwood or any hard-surface material can be used.

Materials like plastic, metal and glass also create more yang features. A room with straight lines, angular shapes, high ceiling and with a lot of metal, light and glass is considered a space with abundant yin properties. In Germany, the Bauhaus era introduced a lot of yang features in architecture. A person who wants to attract yang properties must see to it that he still includes furniture with rounded edges because any sharp-edged furniture is a representation of a weapon in Feng Shui.

Modern architecture, however, isn't natural. Therefore, it is better to bring nature photos, animal prints, plants, wood, earthenware products, shells and water to make the room more inviting. If the room has excessive yang features, the individual can include throw pillows and cushions in earth tones and muted colors. Fabrics can be more detailed. Trees, plants, area rugs and nature art can also be added. The paint can be in a darker and restful color. Furthermore, the lighting can be muted and window coverings can be darker.

It is important for every room to still be balanced. Yin or yang features can be emphasized, depending on the use of the room. If the bedroom is a yang room, the person can't get enough rest. If the home office has a lot of yin properties, the person using it won't be able to finish any work. Therefore, an individual must understand yin and yang principles so that he can apply them in his home to support the lives and needs of everyone living in the house. Balanced rooms in the house can create a harmonious home which nurtures, uplifts and supports the lives of those who live there.

Chapter 7: Create Harmony At Home And in Life Through Feng Shui

The center of the home is considered sacred in Feng Shui. It is where all home energies come from. If this center is kept clean, clutter-free and open, the home is made harmonious and healthy. In Feng Shui, every part of the house is related to a particular area in a person's life. As an illustration, the eastern part of the house is connected to family and health, while the southwest area is responsible for marriage and love relationships.

To apply Feng Shui principles in the home, it is important for the individual to know the Bagua, which is an energy map of the house, which can access the interconnection of the home residents and the physical space. The first step in applying Feng Shui is to clear the clutter to heighten and clear the life energy levels. A clutter-free home is also necessary in enhancing energies.

In the family room, dining room, living room, kitchen and the eastern part of the house, happy pictures of the family can be placed. Feng Shui techniques must also be applied in the bedrooms. The use of harmonious colors can balance the home energies, according to the 5 elements of Feng Shui. The individual must keep in mind his home's EMF level in order to have a healthy home. Energy purifiers like candles, crystals and essential oils can bring balance, calm and harmony into the house.

A happy, beautiful and healthy home, which is shared with loved ones, is truly a blessing to the individual. Family members can live harmoniously in the home by applying Feng Shui cures, which are guaranteed to move energies in the house in order to ensure harmony and balance. In the eastern portion of the house, a fountain can be placed to invite the benevolent Chi in the home. However, the water must be clean at all times. The environment can be balanced by considering the birth element of each member of the family. Dangerous and harsh chemicals in the house must be limited.

A house in harmony can host various activities and people without losing the essence of healing. However, it takes time to create this type of home. The process of applying Feng Shui principles can be condensed into just one principle; a person who loves his home is able to receive more love. As such, the home must be loved without any further delay. The healing potential of Feng Shui can be uncovered if the individual acts today.

Chapter 8: Enhancing Family and Health Through Feng Shui

A person may desire a more wonderful family relationship or a healthier body for himself or for his loved ones. Feng Shui, being concerned with home energies, can help in enhancing somebody's health or family relationship. The applications of Feng Shui are actually obvious, simple, logical and practical, although there are some parts, which are esoteric and mysterious. The Book of Changes or the I Ching is the source of wisdom of the Bagua, a home energy center in Feng Shui.

For the masters of ancient Feng Shui, the home has particular parts, which correspond, to important areas in the lives of its residents. As such, a person can work on the energy centers to identify what's happening in his life and to enhance his life by activating the chi energy. The Book of Changes has been used as a way of realizing the right action. It includes the expressions of the yin and yang to contemplate on the inner development and change process. The Bagua map is used to chart the 9 energy centers of the house. The translation of the Bagua into 8 trigrams includes important areas like wealth, love, self-cultivation, creativity, health, career and fame.

The Zhen is the trigram related to the areas of family and health, although some Feng Shui schools separate family and health into different categories. If problems should arise, the family becomes the support system. The wood element, which is represented by the tree, connects the family and health. The ancestors protect the family and health to retain inner stability, even when trouble arises. Broken circles and relationships are healed within the family. Furthermore, sustenance and money are also dealt within the Zhen. If a family member is poor or someone has health problems, an area of the house can be enhanced.

To enhance the energy center pertaining to health and family, the individual must place objects in the area, which have the most meaning to him. Pictures of landscapes and healthy plants can be hung in the room. It is best to use a picture of a plant or a tree, which the person loves. Affirmations about the person's ideal outcome or health must be written and placed in a box within the area. If he has a problem regarding finances, his affirmations must be about his ability to financially support not only himself but his family as well. The affirmations must include gratitude in the present tense. They can be ended with the phrase, "this, or something better for the good of all concerned."

It is also good to put a healthy plant in the health and family area. If a live plant is not a viable option, pictures will do. Vibrant silk plants are the next best alternative to a live plant. Wooden objects, fabrics, wallpapers and floral prints must be included in the area, along with family heirlooms, which have personal value to the individual. If the person is concerned about a family member's health or relationship, he can include mementos of that person in the area. Furthermore, symbolic pictures of positive relationships and good health as well as personal mementos can be added in the room. Collages and vision boards can be powerful additions as well. Personal objects and artworks of the things he wants for himself and his family can be added. The idea is to make the area more personal so that the positive chi can be created.

If a person is struggling with weight issues, he can search for pictures, which represent his ideal body type. If he's working on self-acceptance, he can hang pictures of himself showing how he enjoys and loves life. He can also make collages of family members he is concerned about and surround them with positive words, trees and vibrant flowers, which depict his vision for them. If he wants somebody to be pregnant, he can have pictures of happy families as an affirmation of his desire. If he's struggling with money matters, the health and family area can be enhanced with money collages and mobiles to represent his ability to sustain himself and his family.

If the person has already identified the health and family area of his home, he should check this area closely. The artwork must be an affirmation of good, vibrant health and joy. Any abstract art or negative artwork, which depicts dismembered body parts must be taken out of the house. Such pieces must be displayed in art galleries. For the home, art should emit joy and happiness. Feng Shui encourages the energy in the physical environment to move the lives of family members forward. Objects with positive personal meanings must be placed in the surroundings to send the chi direction into the home.

To find the personal health and family area in the house, it is important to refer to the Bagua map. To start, a floor plan of the house must be sketched in birds-eye view. Attached garages, stairways and built-on decks must be included. If the occupant is living in a room, an apartment or a condo, he/she has to sketch the shape of his living quarters as if he's looking down from above. A rectangle or square can be drawn to represent the Bagua map so that the whole house is inside that shape. The rectangle or square must be drawn even if the house has an irregular shape. The whole house must be inside the square or rectangle.

Next, the person must stand at the front entrance and the map must be parallel to the floor. The Entrance Quadrant must touch his stomach. This activity will show him the direction of the Bagua map overlay on the floor plan. The house can then be divided into 9 equal sections with the overlaid Bagua map. This process will determine the 9 key areas of the house. The upper left quadrant is the wealth area while the upper right is the love and marriage area, and so on. If the house isn't in the shape of a square or rectangle, it will be missing some Bagua areas. To remedy this, the individual can do it on a per-room basis. Each room can be divided into 9 areas. The wealth corner of each room must be enhanced. The room's main entrance will serve as the front door of the house. If the house is multi-storey, the floor below must be above the Bagua map.

Chapter 9: How To Attain Prosperity Using Feng Shui

As affirmed by the old Feng Shui masters, a person who doesn't strive for wealth doesn't invite wealth in his life. However, Feng Shui provides the important support for him to look for fortune and wealth. By using different Feng Shui principles to establish the environment, the person will be strengthened and he will attract the energies of wealth and prosperity. Traditional Feng Shui makes use of the dragon turtle, the laughing Buddha, Chinese coins, wealth ship, money plant and the wealth vase. These have been used to attract prosperity since time immemorial.

To attract the Wealth Chi, the person must ensure that his home has a strong front door, which symbolizes protection, good luck and abundance when Feng Shui symbols are attached to it. The office and the home must be clutter-free because cluttered space doesn't keep or attract the wealth energy. The person must search for the money area around the house and be sure to take good care of it. If the house has no wealth area because it is of irregular shape or if the bathroom turned out to be the wealth area, he can find the appropriate Feng Shui cures for it. It is also good to use Feng Shui symbols in the home, which personally speak of abundance and wealth. It can be a classical symbol or his representation of wealth energy.

The home or office can be decorated using an aquarium to attract prosperity. There are also wealth crystals available which can be used to attract the wealth Chi. Citrine and pyrite can be displayed together with a Feng Shui gem tree in the wealth corner of the house. Because citrine can also strengthen self-esteem, it can be used as jewelry. Fountains can attract a fresh wealth energy Chi. Even pictures of flowing water can also be used if it's not possible to install a fountain in the house or office. For pictures of water, the individual must ensure that there is an open view and plenty of foam so that it can offer power to the Feng Shui application. The flow of Chi must be regularly checked. If the person wants to attract abundance and wealth energies, he must use different Feng Shui wealth symbols.

Money is energy. In Psychology, money can't fulfill anyone's basic needs. It can be a tool to fulfill the basic needs of mankind. People want money because of what it brings to them. A lot of people have justified emotions with regards to money. Some individuals believe that money makes people corrupt. There are also people who define themselves in terms of how much money they have. Other individuals believe that they will only be secure if they have money. Before organizing the home to attract prosperity, it is important for the individual to clear his mind and emotions of any negative feelings with regards to money.

A person who's struggling with his finances can actually improve his financial standing by enabling his home to support the power of abundance. After getting rid of negative emotions, the person has to free his home from clutter while paying special attention to each room's far left corner. If a person can detoxify, his home can also do it. Any chemical housecleaning products must be thrown away. Natural products must be used to support the home's dynamic energy. Furthermore, Earth-friendly toiletries can be used to limit the amount of toxins that go down the drain and into the Earth. It is also important to clean the windows because doing so is a symbol of new approach to life with a clear mind.

Live plants can detoxify the air. Live and healthy plants can cut down electromagnetic energy in the home, as they are also a symbol of abundance and nature. A jade plant or a money tree can be grown if the individual wants to create abundance. However, any lush, leafy plant can be grown. The kitchen has been a symbol of prosperity since the beginning of time. A person who is well nourished can also be abundant. As such, he is advised to use the kitchen as often as possible. Also, compassion is directly related to prosperity. As such, the person is encouraged to give more to his community and neighbors. Every small donation of even his time counts a lot.

The house must welcome guests. The person must allot a space in the house to receive guests. In that receiving area, he has to have red flowers or pillows to attract more fresh energy and more great people into the home. Because stress can cause stagnation, Feng Shui encourages play to let the energies flow. The person must allot time for his creative pursuits because creativity unlocks one-of-a-kind solutions to problems. In Feng Shui, money and self-empowerment are one and the same. By empowering his home, he is also enriching his own energy and boosting his mood so that his life will turn out to be prosperous.

In traditional Feng Shui, the money area is in the southeast area. On the other hand, the money area is in the upper left corner of the home or office in Western Feng Shui teachings. Although this may sound confusing, the money area in Feng Shui is only one area. The person must decide which Bagua School he will follow. Once he makes a decision, he has to stick to it to encourage continuity and smooth energy flow.

Chapter 10: Clutter And Decluttering

You have come across the term clutter and the term decluttering at least twice in the book. But what is clutter? Have you tried to identify what the clutter in your house is? Have you ever wondered what clutter is? You can pick up the dictionary that is lying at home and look up the word. To make it easier for you, walk up to your living room or your office table. You will find clutter!

Defining Clutter

There are three definitions that have been provided in this section. These definitions give you the best picture of what clutter is!

Clutter is the heap and the pile of the things that you have stopped wanting and needing. These have been accumulated and often cause a lot of disorder in your life.

Clutter is also defined as the item that is perceived as something that is causing a disturbance and interference in your life. These items are what give you immense amounts of confusion. You will be unable to concentrate on what you want most. There may be a lot of things that you have and have forgotten about in this clutter!

Clutter is a luxury. Does that statement surprise you? It may have, but you have to realize that this is the truth. This is a luxury that you are able to afford. You may use this luxury on a regular basis but will forget about it soon after you purchase it. Most psychologists have termed this luxury as an obsession. If you want to have a balance in your life you have to ensure that you do not have an accumulation of this luxury. But you forget, in your excitement, that this luxury affects your entire life.

The third definition of clutter is the most accurate one. But the simplest definition of clutter is that it is a distraction. You forget about what you want in this clutter.

The three types of clutter

There are three types of clutter. You may have worked on organizing your house on so many occasions. During these processes, you may have separated your clutter into different categories. These categories are the three main forms of clutter. This section of the chapter explains these three types of clutter. You will learn how and why this clutter affects you. This clutter ensures that there is no energy that is flowing in your home. This section also helps you identify how you can change all of that. There are three types of clutter – the inner, outer and other clutter.

Inner Clutter

Inner clutter, what could it possibly mean? Do you have any idea? This is the clutter that exists in your brain. It is the clutter that exists inside your ears. You will have to remember that the inner clutter has been with you since you were born. It may have been inside you even before you were born. This is the clutter of your emotions, opinions, thoughts, perceptions and your beliefs towards life and yourself.

You have to remember that you are your greatest threat. The different threats that exist are not the terrorists or the disease cancer. It is you. You know yourself the best and you are the only person who can bring yourself down to the ground. You have let yourself live inside your head and command you. Your inner self is often cluttered and does not know what is good for you and what is not good for you. It is in chaos on every occasion. You will need to step up and take charge before this clutter goes out of control. You will need to be very conscious of the information that is being absorbed by your inner self. You have to ensure that you will need to use all the energy that you use for these thoughts for something worthwhile.

Outer Clutter

This clutter is all the material that you own. You will find that there are certain objects in your home that have taken their spot in the attic or in a corner at home. This is the stuff that you do not require but believe that you require. You keep purchasing these items and finally begin to store them after using them once or never having used them.

Other Clutter

This type of clutter is directly linked to your relationships with the people at your workplace or at your house. If the people in your life did not exist, would you change them in anyway? You may be reluctant to answer this question, but you know that if asked about this when you were alone, you would have said that you would not mind a change.

There are different people in your life who love you for who you are and would not want to change even a hair on your head. These are the people you need to have in abundance. But there are other people around you who are mean and calculative. These are the people you have to try to avoid being around. You have to ensure that you stay away from them. These people use all the positive energy that you need in order to prosper in life. You need to learn to build relationships that are healthy. Only then will you be able to live a happy life. You will also need to draw the boundaries for these relationships. This is only to ensure that you are happy. You will need to ensure that there are certain people that you remove from your life. It is difficult to do this but you have to try.

The three types of clutter are interrelated. You will find that you have to work on each piece of clutter before you have moved onto the next form of clutter. There are times you will have to work on decluttering one form of clutter while working on decluttering another form. This is not a bad thing since you have begun to work on decluttering.

How the types of clutter affect you

As mentioned in the first part of this chapter, clutter is a distraction. This distraction is dangerous and may also be hazardous at times. There are certain drastic effects of clutter.

- Clutter uses all the positive energy that is found in your house.
- You find that the clutter is using up all your time. If you are not looking at it, you are wondering what can be done to remove the clutter.
- You find yourself feeling powerless when it comes to making decisions
- You will find that you are unable to earn any money and will begin to work on spending all the money you own on the outer clutter.
- You will find yourself with a lower amount of money than normal due to the clutter you own
- You will start to perceive yourself negatively
- The plans you may have made for yourself will begin to change drastically.
- You will begin making the worst decisions and choices for yourself.
- You will find yourself judging people and making your opinions about them due to the clutter you own.

Why do we have a lot of clutter?

There are multiple reasons why human beings have a lot of clutter at home. You will be able to come up with numerous reasons why this can happen. This section covers the basic reasons of why a human being clutters. There are other reasons that you may have! Feel free to include those in this list.

1. You have the feeling that if you throw the object out, you will need it the next minute.
2. There are certain things that you find are good enough to use even when they are terribly old and on the verge of breaking.
3. The object that you are looking at is a gift and you do not have the heart to throw it out
4. You may wonder how the person who gave you the gift may feel if they come to your house and do not find their gift
5. If you have item that is expensive, you will worry about the loss of the item and the money
6. You may have items that still have their price tag on!

7. There may be some items at home that are broken. You believe that you can get them fixed.
8. When you have too many clothes that do not fit, you will not throw them away since you will believe that you can wear them when you lose your weight. You need to remember that your clothes have to fit you and that it is not you who has to fit into your clothes.
9. You have clothes that used to be in fashion years ago, but believe that they will come back into fashion
10. You love the item that you have and cannot bear to part with it. This reason is one of the worst reasons possible.
11. You bought it in a sale! You got it for free! Why would you want to get rid of it?

There are multiple other reasons why you may be unable to get rid of the clutter. You can take a sheet of paper and begin to note those reasons down. It is only when you do this that you will be able to get rid of the different clutter.

When some people are asked why they have clutter at home, they have multiple other reasons. You may have given people other reasons too! Do any of these reasons look familiar to you?

1. I am a very busy person. I cannot handle the clutter I have at home after coming from work. I need to finish work before I think about the state of my house.
2. I do not have enough space to store all my belongings. This is the only reason why they are all piled one on top of the other.
3. I need someone to come and help me with sorting the items that I own.
4. I do not know where I am supposed to start.
5. I do not know how this needs to be done
6. If there are systems that can be used to remove clutter, I will need to be taught them since I have no knowledge of those
7. I do not have the finances to buy the system or hire someone to help me organize my house

There are other reasons why you would not want to organize clutter. This is because your mind is telling you that you must not do it!

1. You may claim that you do not have the energy that is required to ensure that you remove the clutter from home
2. You do not have the will power to stick to what you had begun
3. You do not find yourself motivated to work on organizing your house

You and every other human being can relate to these reasons at some point in life.

What is decluttering?

Decluttering is the removing of all the clutter that exists in your life! This is the inner, outer and other clutter. It is essential that you finish this process before you move into organizing your house through the principle of Feng Shui. This is because you will only be able to understand how you can organize your house through Feng Shui when you know what you own! The next chapter helps you understand how this can be done. It provides a seven-step method that you can use to ensure that you have a decluttered home!

Chapter 11: The Seven Steps To Decluttering

As mentioned above, there are seven steps that you will need to follow to ensure that your house is decluttered. The order of the steps can be changed if you want them to. However, it is best if you stick to these steps alone. When you begin the process of decluttering, it is good if you continue it on all the seven days without giving up. Only when you declutter will you be able to find items that you need and arrange your house using the principles of Feng Shui.

Step 1: Rid your house of all its dust!

This is an extremely important step. There is a lot of dust that flows into your house through the wind. This dust gets accumulated in many different crevices and surfaces. If you want to clean your house up, start with the most basic step of all.

You will need to follow a strategy when you are working towards removing the dust from your house. You cannot expect to clean the entire house in one stretch. It is not humanely possible! You can create a schedule for yourself where you will be able to dedicate a certain amount of time to dusting different parts of your house. You can use the divisions that have been provided below to help you structure your plan.

Electronics and gadgets

The different electronic items in your house, like televisions, computers, printers, stereos and many others are the hubs of dust. You have to clean them regularly or you will find that these gadgets are bathed in dust. If you forget about dusting your electronic gadgets, you will cause a huge problem for them. These dust particles may be minute but they cause a lot of harm to the gadgets. They start to clog the electronic items. You will have to use a vacuum cleaner or a cloth that is suitable for the television and the computer to avoid scratching the screen.

Vents

The hinges in your windows and doors and the vents also attract tremendous amounts of dust. You will have to use a very thin cloth to clean this dust. When you are cleaning the window, you can use a liquid.

Ceiling fans

The ceiling fans have a horrible amount of dust on them. You can use a damp cloth and start to clean your ceiling fan. To ensure that the fan is sparkling clean, you can use a tissue. This is your final part of step 1! You have done a commendable job. Now let us move to the next step. Get your step stool, damp a microfiber wiping cloth and clean your ceiling fan. To give the final touch, use a damp paper towel.

Step 2: Clean your bathroom

Now that you have finished dusting your home, you can move into cleaning different parts of your house. You can start off by cleaning your bathroom. You may find it terrible to want to clean your bathroom. But this step is of high importance. You have to ensure that your bathroom is hygienic and does not have germs building up and having families of their own.

Divide the work of cleaning the bathroom too! You can then work easily on cleaning the bathroom.

Clean washroom curtains and mats first

You have mats and curtains in your bathroom. The mats may be filthy. The curtains may have become dirty too! Begin by cleaning those first. It is important that you remove the mats and the curtains and then clean them before you place them back. It is best to have fresh ones placed every week. Ensure that you do not have a pile of junk sitting on the mat.

Dirt free your shower

Your shower is that one place that gets dirty easily. You may have hair that has clogged the drain. This may make you nauseous. You have to step up and clean it before it piles up.

Cleaning of tiles, walls and ceiling

You will need to remember to clean the tiles and the walls. They tend to get dirty. Do not let the dirt pile up and make you feel nauseous. When you come home from work, you want to have a calming bath! Ensure that your bathroom is good enough for the same.

Cleaning sink and bath-tub

The bathtub and the sink need to be very clean. You have to ensure that there is no dirt that has accumulated in either of these places. If there is dirt, then you will have to scrape it off quickly. Otherwise you will find yourself leading a life that is full of filth. You may be leading yourself to obtaining diseases and other infections. Always clean the sink and tub.

Step 3: Cleaning the Kitchen

The place where you cook and store food is the one place that needs to be cleaned on a regular basis. You have to ensure that the place where you obtain nutrition from is 100% clean and has no germs anywhere.

Follow instruction manual to clean appliances

You have a lot of appliances in your kitchen. You will have to keep these clean. You can use the different material that is provided in the instructions to help you clean these appliances. Make sure that your refrigerator and mixer are clean. You cannot have dirty refrigerators since your vegetables and fruits will get spoilt in such conditions.

Cleaning the counter top

You cut and clean your vegetables on your counter top. You have to ensure that you clean the counter top every day. You also place your food on the counter top. It is always good to ensure that this place is disinfected on a regular basis.

Cleaning the floor

The floor needs to be clean at all times! Did you know that in most Asian countries, the people do not walk into their kitchen with their slippers on? This is to ensure that there is no dirt that is being carried into the kitchen. You have to ensure that you kitchen floor is clean since there should be no dirt that can fly into the food when you are cooking.

Step 4: Cleaning the Bedrooms

The bedroom is where you spend time with your family. You relax in this part of your house. When you sleep here, you feel rejuvenated. It is always good to ensure that this part of your house is clean! You want to enter your bedroom and forget all about the tensions during the day. You do not want to be reminded of anything that had caused you any tension during the day. This section helps you work on cleaning your bedroom and removing all the clutter!

Take out all the furnishings and clean them out

Remove all the curtains, linens, mattresses and pillows and dust the, out. You can wash them and leave them to air. Make sure that your mattresses are left out in the sun. This ensures that there is no fungus that will form in your mattress. You can use different cleaners to ensure that you have the cleanest furnishings in your house!

Cleaning cabinets and reorganizing them

You may have a lot of cabinets and shelves in your room. These may have different documents and papers. You can also have clothes and other medicines. You have to ensure that you clean all this out. Empty your cupboards and see what the items you need are and what you do not need. Remove all the items you do not need and give them away to people who will use them. Then arrange all the other items in order.

Clean and polish bedroom furniture

You have to polish all the furniture in your bedroom. Your beds should look as good as new. You may have bedside tables, which also need to be cleaned. You can polish them and ensure that they look brand new! Clean all the lights and the lamps in your room!

Add the tinge of your favorite aroma in your bedroom

It is always good to have an aroma in your room. You may love the smell of lavender. When your room smells the way you want it to, you will be able to relax with ease. You will find that you have an uplifted mood too!

Step 5: Cleaning the Living Room

This is the next most important room of your house! When you have guests over at your place they would love to sit with you in your living room. You have to ensure that this room is clean and tidy. You may have a lot of furniture and fixtures in the room. But do not worry! You can persevere and clean the room up with ease!

Window cleaning

The windows need to be clean all the time. You should be able to look out of the window if you want to. You need to dust the window frames and clean the glasses.

Cleaning of fixtures

You need to ensure that your living room is bright! Adding more lighting in the room can only do this. This would mean that you have a lot of fixtures in your room. You need to clean those too! The dust there will make your living room look dull since the dust will begin to cover the light.

Vacuum clean drapes, blinds and sofas

Your sofa is close to the wall. You know that there will be dust between the wall and the sofa. There will be dust under the sofa as well! Take a vacuum cleaner and eradicate all the dust that is there!

Dust and clean your souvenirs

You may have a lot of souvenirs in your living room. You have to work on dusting them! They are very delicate to clean and you do not have the time to clean all of them up! But you will need to do this! If there is too much dust you will find it very difficult to clean them and may scratch or damage them. To avoid this, you can clean your souvenirs on a regular basis.

Cleaning of your indoor plants

You may have plants inside your house to promote the presence of the Earth elements. You will have to clean these plants on a regular basis. They add beauty to your living room. But if they are not taken care of, you will find that you are causing an imbalance in the energy in your room. You will need to ensure that the plants are clean and that there are no dead leaves and flowers. Ensure that they are not in the room when you are working on sanitizing the room.

Step 6: Cleaning the Floors

This is the penultimate step! You have to ensure that your floor is clean. Try to remove all kinds of dirt from the floor. You may have different types of floors at home. This section helps you cater to all the types of floors!

Cleaning of wood floors

These floors are the best! They add glamor to your house. They are also the best ones to have since they connect you to the earth. You cannot use a lot of chemicals on the wood since that would affect the wood in an adverse manner. You can use the other types of cleaning. You can use a brush to clean the floor.

Tiled/Marble floors cleaning

Marble floors are quite fashionable. Marble is used in bathrooms and been in the kitchen. You have to ensure that you clean your marble floors on a regular basis. Only when they are cleaned will you be able to ensure that there is no dirt in your house! You will have been able to declutter.

Cleaning of ceramic floors

These floors are the easiest to maintain. These are artificial marble and hence do not have the same problems as marble flooring. You can clean them with soft cleansers without having to worry about causing any abrasions.

Cleaning of vinyl floor

Vinyl floors are the simplest floors to clean. Use neutral cleaning liquid. You can mop it on a regular basis to ensure that there is a shine.

Cleaning of brick floors

Brick floors give your house a brilliant look! But they are porous and will have a lot of dirt within them. You will need to dedicate a lot of time to cleaning these types of floors.

Step 7: It is time to Feng Shui

You have worked on decluttering your house. You would have come across many items that you never knew existed! Try using them when you are working on the rearrangement of your furniture. You can always take the help of your family for the same! Ensure that you do it together since that will leave each of your feeling elated. You will have a connection with every part of your house. This will ensure that you clean your house on a regular basis and maintain the balance of energies!

Chapter 12: Feng Shui For Every Room In The House: The Living Room, The Dining Room And The Kitchen

The Living Room

Every homeowner should know that the living room shows his values and the kind of relationship that the people living in the house share.

As a rule, one should get rid of furniture that does not have a happy history. If a piece of furniture fails to uplift one's energy, it is best kept away. Every family member should have a seat in the living room.

Naturally, the arrangement of the furniture should be able to smooth not only the movement of chi but the conversational flow as well. Think of chi and conversation as water and think of the seats as islands. Make sure that the members of the household will be seated in such a way that they will be facing each other.

Backs should be supported from behind and everyone should have a clear view of the door. Arrange all furniture so as to ensure that everyone can see anyone who is entering the living room.

The sofa or any piece of primary furniture is expected to have the command view. To ensure protection, one must ground single seats with side tables. Furniture with sharp angles should be avoided. Furniture with rounded corners is preferred. Likewise, avoid setting up plants with pointed leaves. Also, every homeowner should take measures to ensure that this area of the house is well lit. The good luck zone of the living room is located at the center. Hence, when decorating the living room, one should consider leaving an open space in the center to invite wealth.

Avoid living room designs that consist of an alcove. This will lead to stagnation of positive energy. A mirror on the wall helps add some depth to the room and inspires the movement of energy. Instead of using cabinets that have open shelves, opt for the more traditional bookcases. Be sure to keep the cabinet doors shut at all times because they release negative energy and cause illness. If one has been using an open shelf to hold his books, add some green plants to the shelf to counter the destructive effect. Wooden shelves should not be placed in the southwestern and in the northwestern parts. Neither should they be located in the center part of the living room.

If the living room is situated in the northern part of the house then glass shelves should be avoided. When decorating the living room with family photos, make sure that the images include all of the members living in the house. It's best that all family members look alive and happy in these pictures. Otherwise, they will fail to bring in good luck. To facilitate energy flow, columns should be cut at a 45-degree angle. One may use plants to fill in empty corners.

The Dining Room

The dining room is the part of the house that represents health and nourishment. Therefore, it should be turned into a sacred space. By creating a pleasant atmosphere in one's dining room, the homeowner is showing that he values the life-sustaining chi that he receives whenever he eats.

Generally, dining rooms should foster intimacy and tranquility. Therefore, it is important to ensure that every member of the family has his own comfortable seat in the dining area. Naturally, the dining space should be free from clutter and any artwork should depict a pleasant and appetizing image.

Like in the living room, dining room furniture should have rounded edges. Placing fresh fruit or flowers on the table is also recommended. Clean the table after every meal. And while living room spaces need to be well lit, dining areas should have dimmer lights. It should be just enough for the diners to see the food well. Light should be directed upward. Candelabras with soft illumination may be used. Refrain from hanging ceiling fans directly above the dining room table. Also, avoid using the dining space as a place to keep newspapers or paperwork from the school or the office.

Separate the dining room from the living room and from every other room in the house with a divider. One may also make use of a different color or theme for the dining area so as to distinguish it from the living room. In some cases, a tall houseplant may be used in lieu of a divider. A spacious dining area with a high ceiling tends to foster relaxation in diners. If space doesn't permit it, one can employ decorating strategies to make the ceiling appear higher.

Large mirrors can create a doubling effect on one's utensils and are therefore recommended. Also, it is necessary to make sure that there is an even number of chairs around the dining table. One should avoid placing the dining table in line with the door or the window. One should definitely not place the table between two doors. This will cause happiness and health to flow out of one's home. If the space leaves the homeowner little choice, then hanging Feng Shui wind chimes may help correct the negative effects.

The diners must not be seated in such a way that they are facing towards the bathroom. Not only does it ruin the appetite, it can also affect a person's health. Remember that eating is a time for replenishing the body. Also, the shape of the mats should agree with the shape of the dining table. Simply put, round tables need round coasters. Serving colorless liquid in shiny glasses during mealtime helps attract prosperity and positive energy flow. Lastly, one should avoid utilizing chipped plates and glasses because they invite misfortune into the home.

The Kitchen

Similar to the dining area, the kitchen should be a place for attracting life-sustaining energy. Every time a person cooks, he is honoring the Earth's nourishing resources and attracting abundance. For these reasons, the kitchen requires special attention. It is important that the cooking stove should be kept clean and all of its burners should be used on a regular basis. Some people have this habit of using only one or a couple of the burners frequently while neglecting the rest. If one likes to cook, he should provide a commanding view for himself by placing a mirror above the stovetop. Alternatively, one may use reflective pots. This is to make sure that the cook gets a clear view of what's behind him.

Preferably, the kitchen should be airy and clutter-free. It should give off the impression of warmth and energy because that energy will be passed on to the food and the food's energy will be passed on to the person. Bright and cheerful colors for the walls are recommended. Cooking with gas stimulates abundance as opposed to cooking with electricity. This is because by cooking with gas, one is utilizing the fire element. Potted herbs, fruits and flowers are also advised for the kitchen. Cabinets and countertops should be kept well organized.

As with the dining area and the living room, kitchen furniture should have curved or rounded designs. Remember that sharp edges harbor negative energy. If there are items in the kitchen that the cook does not utilize every day, then they are best kept inside closed storage spaces. After working, one should immediately get rid of the trash. In fact, if possible, the kitchen should be cleared before eight in the evening. Make sure that the garbage bin is empty during the night. A kitchen should be free of photographs of family and friends. There are some people who like placing images of loved ones on the refrigerator and kitchen countertops and this should be avoided. Minimize the use of fluorescent lights and as much as possible, try to obtain natural lighting. As with the dining room, broken utensils should be thrown away. Hoarding useless objects in the kitchen will only bring about stagnation of energy flow.

The most ideal place to build a kitchen is at the back of the house where visitors and strangers cannot see it as they come into one's home. To separate the kitchen from the entryway, one may place decorative curtains that can take a person's eyes away from the kitchen. Low storage cabinets are preferable to large cabinets mounted into walls. Another thing that a homeowner should avoid is situating the kitchen sink beside the stove. This is because the stove represents the fire element while the sink represents the water element. As an appliance representing the water element, the fridge should not be placed beside the stove either. In fact, the stove and the refrigerator should be at least six feet away from each other. If one's stove or sink is trapped in a corner, a good solution would be to build a kitchen island.

Mirrors and glossy wall tiles helps attract prosperity, brighten up the room and make the space seem bigger. Knives have sharp edges so unless they are being used, they should be kept inside a closed cabinet or in a knife holder. Lastly, keep in mind that the kitchen symbolizes both health and wealth so couples and family members are encouraged to use this area.

Chapter 13: Feng Shui For Every Room In The House:

The Bathroom

Every homeowner must keep in mind that the bathroom is a place for cleansing and renewal. Therefore, one should make sure that the bathroom design invites vitality, and encourages the letting go of things that no longer have a purpose.

As a general rule, bathrooms should be well lit and well ventilated. Installing plants can help in purifying the air. Needless to say, the bathroom should always be clean and free from clutter. It should smell good and if one wishes to hang images in the bathroom, the images should remind him of rejuvenation and purification. The bathroom is filled with water elements so to balance it out; a person may add some wood elements. Faceted crystals may be added to improve the overall energy in the bathroom.

Keep in mind that the flow of energy is similar to the flow of money. Inside the bathroom, the toilet, the sink and the tub are holes through which money can pour out. This is why the drains should be closed when one isn't using them. The toilet lid must always be kept down and the door must always be kept closed. Avoid placing the toilet on the southwestern part of the house. If one builds the bathroom on the southern part of the home, this can disturb the existing harmony between family members. One should also refrain from placing it on the northwestern part. Otherwise, this will create negative effects to the residents' wellbeing. One should also avoid placing the bathroom in the middle of the house. This brings about loss of money.

Building the bathroom near the front door is not a good idea. This will encourage damage to the family's reputation. Bathrooms, in general, should not be situated in the wealth areas of the house. In fact, bathrooms should not be visible from the main door of the home. When installing a bathroom on the second floor, it should not be directly above the main door. Avoid dark designs for the bathroom or have windows and large mirrors fitted. The toilet should not be in line with the bathroom door. To conceal the toilet, make use of curtains, decorative screens and dividers.

The bathroom door should not be visible when one is standing by the kitchen stove. Also, make sure that the bathroom floor is elevated. Avoid setting up bathrooms directly across the stairs. Though the rectangular bathtub is a quite popular, bathtub in the shape of a semi-circle, a circle, or an oval attracts more wealth because they follow the curve of a lucky coin. A homeowner should choose among these shapes if he wishes to attract wealth. Use shells to decorate the bathroom because they symbolize wealth. If one wishes to install a water fountain inside the bathroom, then it should not be located near the toilet. This kind of placement tends to attract failure in one's endeavors.

The Laundry Room

Like the bathroom, laundry rooms tend to have a negative reputation in Feng Shui. This is because they harbor stagnant and cluttered energy. The laundry room should not be placed beside the bedroom. Likewise, it is not advisable to set up large storage areas near the bedroom. A laundry closet should not be positioned facing the main door of the house.

The Home Office/ the Study Room

The main objective for the home office or the study area is to enable the occupant to feel inspired and to facilitate the flow of ideas. The design should be geared towards promoting clarity and productivity. Just like any other room in the house, the home office should be clutter-free. The desk must be located in a power position. This means that one should set the desk where one can see the door, where there is a constant flow of energy and where the people entering are instantly visible. However, one should refrain from situating the desk directly in front of the door. Doing so would be to put oneself directly into the stream of too much energy.

One should sit on a high-backed chair. Or he should make sure that there's a wall directly behind him for support. Windows facing one's back is not good because it causes the person to feel a lack of support. This can be remedied by using drapes and furniture.

Hanging images and inspirational words around the home office or the study area can help motivate the person. However, make sure that these images and mottos are connected with business and not with family life. Otherwise, they are more likely to serve as distractions.

Create an inspiring view from across the desk. If the desk is facing an empty wall, it makes the person feel as though he is lacking in vision and in opportunities. Opt for furniture with rounded edges to minimize the presence of stress in the room. Otherwise, soften sharp edges with the use of fabric. If the sharp edges of an object are sitting directly from across from the person, it should be moved elsewhere because it cuts off the person's energy.

The most important rule of all is that the home office and the study room should be separated from the personal aspects of the homeowner's life. Ideally, they should be in a separate room but if this isn't possible, then make use of dividers and screens. Home office doors and study room doors must be kept shut while one is working. Make sure that one is unable to see the rest of the house. To enhance one's chi, one should dress for success even while working at home. A brief ritual to disconnect home energy from work energy may be done. This can be as simple as lighting a candle. Items used for business and personal items should be stored separately. One should definitely refrain from using the dining table as a study desk or a working desk. Also, bookshelves should not be overloaded. It makes an individual feel overwhelmed and hence, it is counter-productive. Heavy boxes on the floor are also likely to weigh a person down.

Chapter 14: How to Attract Health, Balance And Prosperity While Sleeping

Next to the front door, the bedroom is the most crucial Feng Shui area. Having sufficient rest and sleep is necessary for a person's wellbeing. That being said, the quality of rest and sleep is also important and it is greatly affected by how the resting and sleeping environment is arranged. More than that, an optimal arrangement of the bedroom also yields positive effects in the relationship between spouses. A restful evening leads to a more productive day. When arranged properly, a person's bedroom can even be a means to attract and preserve wealth even while one sleeps. Keep in mind that apart from being a space for regeneration, the bed is where people stay when they are in their most vulnerable state. The body at its sleeping state is rendered defenseless when surrounded by negative energy.

The first thing to consider is the bed's relationship to the door. The most ideal Feng Shui placement is when the person's bed is not in line with the bedroom door. Another recommended location for the bed is placed in the center, on a wall diagonal to the bedroom door. One may also opt to install the bed on the far left wall to achieve the command location. This favorable position enables the body to experience more support while it is at rest.

One thing to definitely be aware of is the death placement. To avoid this unfavorable placement, refrain from situating the bed opposite to the bedroom door. Placing the bed in line with and opposite to a bathroom door is just as dangerous. Positioning one's bed this way may not only lead to disturbed sleeping patterns but also to serious physical illnesses. If one's bed shares the same wall with a sink or a toilet, this can drain not only one's energy but his wealth as well. Remember that toilet flushing represents the flow of fortune out of the household.

No matter how limited the available space, homeowners should also avoid placing the head of the bed directly beside a door. The reason for this is there is simply too much energy flowing in from the room towards the bed. This places the sleeper at risk for developing abdominal discomfort. Also, people who sleep in beds positioned in this manner are more prone to anxiety and anger. If the head of the bed shares the same wall as that of the bedroom door, this causes the person to attract a steady succession of bad luck in his life. Eventually one will find himself dealing with another problem even before the previous one has been resolved. This kind of placement is sure to usher in financial difficulties as well as conflict with family members.

Feng Shui for Beginners: A Complete Guide to Using Feng Shui to Achieve Balance, Harmony, Health and Prosperity in Your Home and Life! – 3rd Edition

There is nothing wrong with selecting beds based on their aesthetic qualities. However, keep in mind that most ornate beds are not able to provide a person with sufficient support. Frames, headboards and nightstands made from metal will make one vulnerable to headaches and head ailments. Avoid positioning beds beneath a window because this does not give the sleeper any support. In fact, sleeping beneath a window causes a person's energy to escape. Instead of feeling invigorated after a nap or a night's sleep, one is likely to feel the opposite. One should then opt for a plain flat wall, which will allow him to take advantage of all the energy that passes by. If, however, a person has no other place to put the bed in, then a drape must be placed on the window. It should be thick and heavy enough to provide the sleeper with a feeling that a wall is located behind him because walls behind the bed symbolize protection.

Wood represents strength and will provide a person with the needed support as he sleeps. When choosing a wooden headboard, make sure that it is around 1.2 to 1.5 meters high. A wooden headboard with cloth inlays may also be chosen. The important thing is that it is maintained parallel to the bedroom wall.

It is also important to determine one's kua number so that he may place the bed in such a way that his head is pointing towards his personal wealth direction. If one's personal direction, however, is in conflict with the basic rules of bed Feng Shui, one may disregard the personal number and instead, follow the proper bed placement. If the space allows it, and if it's in one's wealth position, try placing the bed on two walls opposite to one's bedroom door. This kind of placement is a great way to increase one's finances and attract more business opportunities.

Floral patterns have long been a popular design for bedrooms. However, very few married people know that designs that include flowers and plants can drain sexual energy away from their spouse. While growing plants may be good for other parts of the house, plants and flowers are not good for the sleeping area because they release carbon dioxide at night and prevent a person from taking in positive energy as he sleeps.

Individuals and couples are advised to avoid sleeping and resting in places where water is either visible or audible, whether it is from a leaking sink or an outdoor fountain. Mirrors located on top of the bed, in front of the bed, or anywhere where the sleeper can observe himself while resting should also be avoided. Remember that mirrors are active stimulators and hence, they lessen the quality of the resting space. Husbands and wives should avoid mirrors in which they can see themselves climbing in and out of bed. This provides the illusion of other people climbing in and out of a couple's intimate area. This can lead the couple to engage in affairs, thus, weakening the foundation of the home. Instead, keep the mirror inside a closet door.

Feng Shui for Beginners: A Complete Guide to Using Feng Shui to Achieve Balance, Harmony, Health and Prosperity in Your Home and Life! – 3rd Edition

There has been a huge debate as to whether it is advisable to place a television inside the bedroom. Vintage televisions consist of a rounded glass and when switched off, they resemble mirrors. For this reason, they are not recommended to be placed inside the bedroom. However, flat screen televisions do not pose that same threat. Melancholic paintings and violent art should be kept outside the bedroom. In fact, they are not endorsed to be kept inside the house at all. As mentioned in the earlier chapters, it is better to choose images that reflect harmony and beauty.

Placing lamps symmetrically on both sides of one's bed helps achieve a sense of balance. Even one's sleeping positions can help attract harmony in the household. Keep in mind that the Yang is the masculine side while the Yin is the feminine side. For married couples, it is advised that the woman sleeps at her husband's right side. This shows that she supports him and shares in his job in keeping the household together. This also demonstrates a balanced partnership.

People for extra storage usually use the space underneath the bed. In fact, beds with pullout compartments have long been popular among households. While this may help a homeowner maximize his space, these items beneath the bed can weigh him down as he sleeps. Not only that, they prevent the energy from flowing freely so that it is unable to encircle the person. Spaces underneath the bed should therefore be kept clean and clear of any items with the exception of certain Feng Shui cures.

Feng Shui cures can also help a person in dealing with specific issues. If one has insomnia, placing a tortoise figure beneath the bed can help him sleep better. For the person who is frequently experiencing backaches upon waking up in the morning, this can be cured by placing a few sticks of chalk in a bowl of rice and keeping it under the bed. For individuals who feel that they have been stuck in one place for so long, placing a conch shell beneath the bed will help attract more opportunities for travel. For couples that are worried about fading intimacy, a canopy may be placed over the bed.

One may place a wealth bowl beneath the bed to attract money. As mentioned in the previous chapters, precious stones can help attract prosperity. One may place them under the bed. Alternatively, one can keep a wealth vase or a jewelry box beneath his bed. By doing so, the person is able to achieve more control of the existing fortune while attracting more money towards him/her.

How to Make a Wealth Bowl
A wealth bowl is a great way to stimulate the flow of income and increase one's career opportunities. Compared to the wealth vase, it is much easier to make since it utilizes items that can easily be found in one's home. A person can either place the wealth bowl beneath the bed, in the living room, or near the cash register if one's source of livelihood

is business. The first step would be to choose the right kind of bowl. The recommended type is a crystal bowl or a glass bowl with a round shape. They are better able to hold the items inside. It should be medium-sized or about 8-10 inches wide.

As for choosing the items inside the wealth bowl, a person doesn't have to worry at all about not owning any genuine jewelry. Faux jewels and gold are perfectly fine. One should think of all of the things that signify wealth and prosperity. It can be gold ingots, real or faux diamonds, money, or semi-precious stones like quartz, lapis and amethyst. One may take some soil from a successful business establishment, seal it in a red envelope and add it to the bowl. He may also collect water from that wealthy establishment, place it in a tiny glass bottle, and add it to the wealth bowl. After arranging all of the items in the bowl, fill in the spaces by inserting some lucky Chinese coins. Make sure that the bowl is full to symbolize abundance. If in need of more fillers, gold-painted pebbles will also work.

The next step would be to add in a wealth tree, which can easily be obtained in Feng Shui shops. After placing the wealth tree in the bowl, adorn it with coins, gems and gold nuggets on top. Then get a happy Ho Tai Buddha and add it to the wealth bowl. The golden Buddha will watch over the wealth bowl and help in increasing one's riches.

Lastly, one should know his Chinese zodiac sign and add a figure of his sign to the wealth bowl. Doing so will instill prosperity chi into the bowl.

Feng Shui for Beginners: A Complete Guide to Using Feng Shui to Achieve Balance, Harmony, Health and Prosperity in Your Home and Life! – 3rd Edition

Chapter 15: Feng Shui And The Meaning Of Colors

Color is movement and each color moves according to its own rhythm. A person is connected to the colors of his home through various intersecting energy fields. This makes Feng Shui colors a very powerful element that affects the overall energy of a room.

Consider the house as a gateway to a person's internal and external realities. By looking at an individual's home, one gets a glimpse of where that person is at the present and where that person intends to be in the future. Understanding the basic meaning of colors will help a homeowner determine which colors are most suitable for each room in the house, and which colors are best matched for the specific areas in the Feng Shui Bagua.

Fire Element Colors

The color red has the ability to make a person feel energetic. Crimson and scarlet are stimulating hues. They are also powerful and passionate shades. In Feng Shui, such colors facilitate transformation. They attract not only love and romance but luxury as well, making them perfect for the Bagua areas concerned with relationships and love, abundance and prosperity and fame and reputation. The best places to use red in the home are in the kitchen and in the dining room. Red is also a good color for the living room. Because red stirs energy, add tiny touches of the color in workspaces. However, one should utilize this color in moderation. Otherwise, it can attract anger. When used as a color for the bedroom, go for reds with more earthy tones such as country redwood and Navajo red.

Orange also represents the fire element though compared to red its effect is less arousing. Nevertheless, orange is a very sociable color. It is active and stimulating and because it is less powerful, it is a better color choice for interior spaces. Also, since it is a combination of color, orange is best for places where one is trying to achieve unity and collaboration. For this reason, it is often used in the fame and reputation area of the Bagua. It is also a good color for the dining room because it encourages conversation and appetite. Just like red, when using orange for the bedroom, opt for the more earthy orange tones.

When selecting a color for the abundance and prosperity areas of the Bagua, it is wise to select an uplifting hue such as yellow. It will increase one's mental concentration and productivity and enhance one's memory. It is preferable for the study or for the home office. Yellow is a very happy color and represents light and connection, making it good for the fame and reputation area of the Feng Shui Bagua. If one is trying to achieve harmony, paint the living room, the dining room, or the kitchen yellow. However, one should be careful about using yellow as a main color for the bedroom. It can intensify jealousy and insecurities. This color is also not suitable for other areas of relaxation like the bathroom.

Pink is a fire element color that embodies love and romance and thus, it is recommended for the Feng Shui bagua's relationships and love area.

Purple symbolizes nobility and is linked with the realm of higher consciousness. It is also a very spiritual color and it is to be used when a person is preparing himself to assume a great responsibility. Since the color also signifies wealth, it is advised to be used for the abundance and prosperity areas of the Bagua. Lavender hues and other lighter purples may be chosen for the bedroom to encourage romance.

Earth Element Colors

Though strong yellow is a fire color, light yellow is an earth color. If one is intent on having a yellow-colored bedroom or bathroom, settle for a paler shade of yellow to avoid the fear aggravating effects of bright yellow.

Among the colors, brown is the best representative of simplicity and stability. It is grounding and comforting and is frequently used in the skills and knowledge area of the Bagua. Shades of brown can also be used for the bedroom or the living room.

Wood Element Colors

Green is a very calming color that facilitates healing and invites good fortune. It symbolizes growth and life. As such, the most ideal places to use green are in the health area and in the family and elders area of the Bagua. It can be used as a primary color for the living room and the family room. Because green also represents purification, it is an ideal color for the bathroom. And since it also promotes mental equilibrium, it is recommended for the skills and knowledge area of the Bagua.

Water Element Colors

Blue is a watercolor that produces a calming effect. More than that, it embodies honesty and dependability. Because it stimulates learning and is able to provide a person with clarity, it is a recommended color for the skills and knowledge area of the Bagua. Symbolizing inspiration and flow, blue is also a sound choice for the Feng Shui Bagua areas concerned with abundance and prosperity as well as career and journey. Deep blue accents are advised to be included in bedrooms in order to facilitate sleep. If a person is suffering from anxiety, blue is a good bedroom color for him. Blue is a nice bathroom color as well.

Black is another water element color that promotes tranquility. If a homeowner wishes to achieve focus, he can use black because it absorbs all colors. More than that, black also signifies power and sophistication, making it an ideal accessory color for the skills and knowledge area and the career and journey area of the Bagua.

Metal Element Colors

White connotes purity, innocence and hope. It is an ideal color for the creativity and children's areas of the Bagua. Since it also symbolizes vastness and spirituality, it may be used as a color for the helpful people and travel area of the Feng Shui Bagua. Being a sign of cleanliness, white is a great color for one's bathroom. However, homemakers should be careful about using white as a leading color for a room. It can reduce the flow of chi and the person's ability to think openly. It subjects individuals to prejudice. To avoid this, try adding colors to white as opposed to going for an all-white effect.

Grey, like black, is frequently used as an accessory color instead of a predominate color. It is a calm and conservative color though it lacks vitality. It is most often used in the skills and knowledge area and in the helpful people and travel area of the Feng Shui Bagua. However, the use of grey must be minimal because too much of it may a drain a person of his physical energy.

In selecting colors for the rooms in the house, one should consider its effects to his physiological wellbeing. A homeowner should go with colors that resonate with his personality. Lastly, one should learn to trust his intuition and opt for colors that inspire him as well as other people that reside in the home. For example, if one is told that green is good for healing but he couldn't stand the sight of it, then he should choose a color that makes him feel happy and comfortable.

Chapter 16: Main Entry and Front Door Feng Shui

Up till yet, the book has talked about all the numerous possibilities that one can look for in order to arrange your home in way that enhances the elements and energy of Feng Shui. A good design of the main entry and front door, one which compliments the energy of Feng Shui is very important as both the main entry and front door serve as the opening to the house and as a path for the energy to flow in.

Important elements are to be considered if the entry and door are to provide a smooth, easy absorption for all the energy that comes in. To begin, focus on what aspects you should avoid, and what elements of Feng Shui you should incorporate.

So how do you figure that out?

Try all the possible elements and figure out if an elements and its energy works for you or not. Read and find out related information on Feng Shui energies and elements, if you are still unable to properly understand how to do it, get help from an expert or practitioner.

To make it easier for you, here are a few designing ways that can help you maintain good Feng Shui:

Main Entry

A good Feng Shui through the main entrance ensures that you have a positive Feng Shui energy in your house as well.

Hence is important that you try and encourage the flow of positive and good energy through the main entry.

The main entry is through where the energy flows in, where the absorption of the Chi takes place. When the house experiences a nourishment and flow of good energy right from the opening, it is able to circulate it all around as well. This impacts the people living in the house in a positive way, they start feeling and experiencing a higher level of happiness, health and success.

A good main entry will welcome and attract the energy, and even nurture it, so that it is able to disseminate itself through the entire house. If the main entry energy is weak and does not compliment the energy coming in, then it can push it away.

Feng Shui for Beginners: A Complete Guide to Using Feng Shui to Achieve Balance, Harmony, Health and Prosperity in Your Home and Life! – 3rd Edition

Implement the ways given here in maintaining a good Feng Shui in the main entry and make sure that your door also corresponds with it. As neither can work well if one does not match the other's energy.

Here are some of those ways:

-Bagua is a critical element of the Feng Shui. Find out the bagua are of the main entry and use the appropriate colors and object to enhance the energy of the Feng Shui element. The elements of Feng Shui and their colors have been discussed in the book earlier; match them with the bagua energy in the area to maintain a stronger Feng Shui energy in the main entry.

Whether you use darker colors like red and blue or lighter shades of white or yellow, find out what the bagua area of your main entry is and then match the color accordingly.

-The 'landing space' of your main entry is an important one. Try to create a space that is spacious and welcoming so that it can attract the energy towards it. Focus the décor in the room in a way that it facilitates the smooth flow of energy. There are many choices of Feng Shui décor that one can opt for to build a good Feng Shui in the area. Small, centered lamps with side tables or a big round table placed near the hallway. You can place pots with plants and flowers in vases to bring out the positive vibe in the main entry.

There are many viable choices for décor; the idea is to arrange it in a way that the Chi is welcomed in to your home. Even if the space is small and does not allow for elaborate décor, try to fit in a simple small rug or some colorful objects that appear vibrant and appealing. Sometimes even if you hang a painting or just focus on the wall, it can bring out the good Feng Shui energies.

-Find out about all the things that can bring in a negative energy and avoid those. There are certain objects, colors or décor arrangement that can bring in negative energy, try to avoid such 'Feng Shui disasters'. While trying to establish a good Feng Shui energy in the main entry, you can be faced with certain challenges, what are they and how will you overcome those?

Here are a few examples; there is a mirror facing the main door. This is not a good placement of the mirror. We will talk more about mirror placement in detail later, but with regard to the main entry, if there are any mirrors that face the main door, you must try and change their placement.

Another example would be of a huge wall close to the main entry. This would block and push back all the energy that flows in from the front door. It might be difficult to remove a wall on its own, so try incorporating its energy within the energies of the main entry and door. Other concerns for Feng Shui can rise over bathrooms and stairway placements. If the bathroom is right over the main door, it can pose as a hindrance to all the energy coming in. Similarly, if the staircase is close to the door or facing it, it will not harbor the energy or retain it. Easy solutions to these two respectively would be to contrast the colors from different elements of the two spaces or try and match their energies with each other so that it is nurtured and enhanced instead of being pitted against each other.

Consistency is key, be disciplined and consistent in your efforts to create a good Feng Shui in your home. For that, you must start with the main entry. Try and look for creative décor and colors that match the elements of the Feng Shui in the area and then incorporate it with its bagua energy. You will see the difference yourself. In a few days the vibe and energy will not only be positive around the house but will also help better the living conditions of the people in the house.

Front Door

For a strong Feng Shui influence on the main entrance, one needs first and foremost, focus on the front door. As talked about earlier as well, the door is vital to the flow of energy. Whether it is a home, or a business, the door through which the energy is absorbed from, is integral to the Feng Shui that follows inside. The healthier, more positive and stronger balance of Feng Shui that the door is able to maintain, the better and positive will be the impact of the energy that surrounds the people in the house.

The big question here is; how can you create a stronger influence from Feng Shui? And how can the door of the house help with?

Front doors are considered a very important aspect of Feng Shui. It is called the opening of the 'Chi', its mouth. This signifies that it is the place through which a home receives its energy from and hence it is critical that the energy that passes through to the house is good energy and carries positive vibes.

Here are a few key points to consider when you are focusing on building up on the door:

-Make sure that the pathway in front of the door is clear and has no obstructions. To maintain an open and smooth flow of energy to the door, remove all barriers and blockades such as recycle bins, huge stones and pots, along with any other thing that could be posing as an obstruction in the way of the door. One of the best Feng Shui energy comes from a clean, fresh environment. Hence, try to make sure that it is provided.

One of the ideal pathways would be something that is formed in a flow, and waves in like a fall of water. Not like the straight, sharp paths that you see in modern and recently constructed houses.

-A properly maintained front door is also integral to maintaining good energy. The better cared a front door is, the more are its chances of attracting good, positive energy. Try to make sure that there are less scrapes and marks on it; it has been painted well and there is no peeling of wood or paint anywhere. Also try to avoid squeaky hinges and rust settling in on the door.

Improvise on the ideas given here do what makes the door appear in top notch condition. If you are able to follow this, then you are already halfway on to bringing in a loving and healthy energy into your home.

-The direction of the door and the color should be correlated. The importance of direction in Feng Shui has been emphasized time and again. It is imperative that one chooses the color from the element that relates to the direction that the door is facing.

Figure out and measure the direction that your front door faces, and then color it according to the element that harmonizes with it. For example, the direction of North is surrounded by the element of water; now choose your colors according to this element if your door points towards this particular direction.

-Try to match the energy in the main entry with the door. If the door is enabling a good Feng Shui, then match it up with a smooth flow of energy in the main entry as well. The door cannot be of much help if the energy flowing in follows into a space that does not corresponds with it.

To circulate and harness that good energy within the entire house, make sure that the Feng Shui in the main entry is also maintained the same way, as it is the start to the rest of the house.

-A front door should be proportional with the size of the house. It is a common structural mistake when the size of the door does not match with the overall size of the house. Sometimes small houses can have gigantic, spacious doors, while the bigger houses can have smaller doors compared to their size. If you want to ensure a good Feng Shui door, try and get it build proportional to the size of your house.

Try to maintain a positive vibe and energy around the door, try to get everything to harmonize and balance each other out. This is a crucial aspect of building a good Feng Shui influence.

Feng Shui for Beginners: A Complete Guide to Using Feng Shui to Achieve Balance, Harmony, Health and Prosperity in Your Home and Life! – 3rd Edition

Front Door Colors

If you find yourself confused about what's the right color for your front door now that you know how important it is to let in good energy around the entire house, here's what you can do. Observe the direction that your door faces and then pick the color. It is a tradition in classic Feng Shui that the direction of the door and the color should be corresponding.

Here is some information regarding that:

-If your door faces east, your Feng Shui colors could be brown or green. The East area in in the Feng Shui is associated with the element of wood, thus the colors should also match that element. However if neither green nor brown looks good with your house's color scheme and exterior, then you can opt for other choices as well. Feng Shui gives a lot of choice to people when it comes to home décor and color schemes. Similarly, with the door also, it gives the choice to choose from two other elements.

The elements of water and earth are both known for nurturing and supporting the element of wood. Hence one can make the choice for going with either of the two elements' colors.

These include; blue and black for water, and, light shades of yellow as well as all earthy shades of colors.

Some of the colors, you should absolutely avoid, like purple, red, gray and white. These colors are from the elements of fire and metal, and both do not make a good combination with wood.

However if your door is already painted and cannot be done again, then do not worry. Focus on making the other aspects of Feng Shui work.

-Doors facing Southeast.

The doors that face this direction can be painted of the same color as an east facing door. Their element is the same, wood, and hence some of the same colors can be used here too. The only small difference here is that the Southeast direction is one that is known for harboring wealth and prosperity, so if you are looking to increase that energy, you can opt for blue and black as well. These choices are similar to those of the east facing direction, but the Feng Shui energy of bagua that is applied here, is of money and wealth. Hence to build on that, you can choose the colors from the water or earth element.

-South facing doors.

This direction is the only one that faces the Feng Shui element of fire. Here, yes, you can use the color red to paint the front door. Fire element is associated with the color of red and orange as stated in one of the earlier chapters. Red is indeed the best choice of colors one can go with if their doors face the Southwards direction. Other colors that can also be viable here are strong shades of pink or magenta, yellow and purple.

If neither of these colors, including red and orange go well with the color contrast and exterior look of the house then you can choose some of these as well. Go for either green and brown or a strong yellow color. These colors are attached to the element of wood, and it is responsible for supporting the energy of the fire element.

The colors to avoid here are from the elements of earth and water.

-Doors that face Southwest

The energy that compliments the Southwest direction is of love and maternal warmth, as well as that of marriage. Then the colors that can best help enhance that energy is of the element of earth and include all earthy shades. You can even choose the color of sand or a few from the element that nurture the energy of the earth.

Fire is most supportive to the element of earth and hence you can opt for colors like pink, red, orange, yellow and purple. The best ones would obviously be yellow, sandy or earthy shades but if they do not match with the overall look then you can choose either of the others.

The colors to avoid would be white, grey, green and blue.

-West facing doors

The optimal color choices for a west facing door would be the ones that are associated with the element of metal. The colors include white and gray. These colors correspond with the begun energy of Fang Shun that is related to the direction. This would be the energy of creativity and young children.

The element that works well together with the metal element is earth since it is responsible for creating it. The colors that you should try staying away from are blue, black, dark pink and red.

-Doors in the Northwest direction

The doors in the northwest direction can also be of similar color choices as the west facing doors. Both are of the direction that is complimented by the same Fang Shun element of metal. The difference is of the energy that is associated with this, while the energy in the west is of creativity and children, the northwest direction has the energy of helpfulness surrounding it. Hence some attention to detail is required here. If white or gray cannot be applied on the door, stick to sandy and light yellow colors. These are the colors of the element of earth that compliments metal and helps enhance the positive aura and energy.

Again, be careful to not choose either red or black as these are colors that will work against the energy of helpfulness and blessedness.

-North facing doors

Front doors, which are in the direction of north, are surrounded by the Fang Shun element of water. Interestingly enough, this direction is the only one to be associated with the element of water. The colors that you can use if your front door is in this direction are black and blue.

If you feel uneasy about having a blue or black door or it does not compliment the look of the house, then you can also go for lighter colors from the element of metal. The begun energy that comes with the north direction is of career and life path.

The element of metal also goes well with the energy too. So if you are hesitant about the water element colors of black and blue, you can opt for shades of white and gray. The metal element enhances the element of water and hence is a good secondary option to choose from. Also note that colors such as green, yellow, red and magenta should be kept away.

-Front doors facing Northeast

A door, which faces the direction in the northeast, is carrying the energy of spiritual cultivation and growth. The element that dominates this direction is the element of earth. To enhance the energy of growth and spirituality, colors from the element of earth should be chosen as the element corresponds with the energy.

These colors are light yellow and earthy sandy shades. Fire is another element that compliments the earth element. Hence, if you are looking for another option, you can choose from fire element colors such as red, deep orange and if you are feeling adventurous, even purple.

Do not go for colors from elements that work against the energies here. These would be green and white, brown and black. These are colors from elements of water, wood or even metal. These may not compliment the energy that is accompanied with the direction and may affect it negatively.

Feng Shui for Beginners: A Complete Guide to Using Feng Shui to Achieve Balance, Harmony, Health and Prosperity in Your Home and Life! – 3rd Edition

These are the colors and their elements along with the corresponding directions. Apply them to create an effective Fang Shun door and strengthen its energy.

Front Door Décor

For some reason or the other if you are unable to match the color of your door to its corresponding direction, do not worry. If you cannot repaint it or there is some other problem, you can still ensure a good Fang Shun door. It may take more effort on your part and creativity, but the results in the end will be very satisfying.

There are a number of ways through which one can create an impressive appealing doorway. Designs range from vintage oriental doors with detailed and intricate carvings to modern doors with bright vibrant colors that give a very positive vibe. So you have a lot of choice to work from.

Fang Shun, even in this day and age makes us realize the appeal and importance of the doorway that also functions as a gateway.

The door is important in inviting the right kind of energy in, and keeping the negative unwanted energy out. Hence it is important that it only retains and harbors the good energy that builds up a strong Fang Shun.

You have read earlier about the importance of direction and colors, and ways to maintain a smooth flow of energy in.

The first and easy way to making a strong Fang Shun door is obviously painting it. As stated earlier, find out what direction it faces and then discover the element that dominates that direction. The five elements of water, fire, wood, earth and metal all come with their particular colors, objects and images. The easiest way to harness the energy of the begun and enhance the Fang Shun effect would be to just paint the door of the color from the element corresponding with the directions.

All of the direction with their related elements and colors are given above.

However, when you have figured out that the painting of the door cannot be done according to the direction and element; then what do you do?

You go for the next best décor move.

You use objects, shapes and other things that help nourish the energy of the doorway.

If your door is facing east or southeast, you might want to stick to the colors of green and brown, all earthy shades, since the Fang Shun element that surrounds this direction is wood. And all these colors are symbolic of this particular element. If you can't use it in painting the door, you can use plants, rocks, etc. This will help you in harboring the particular energy of the element effectively.

Use vibrant and fresh plants; decorate with lush greenery and flowers. Try to get pots of earthy colors or in black or blue. Get a doormat in a rectangular shape made from jute. If you have the means for it, install a water fountain that is close to the entrance. And use stones and rocks that are rectangular and square shaped for decoration. That will help build upon the energy of earth.

Note that fire and metal elements do not go well here. Try avoiding metal items and pots, and objects or colors of red, pink, etc.

A south facing door compliments the element of fire. Decorate with objects shaped like stars or triangles. Also use the help of greenery and plants. Here, if you use pots, get them in colors of red, purple or magenta. You can use a rectangular shaped jute doormat for this as well.

Avoid the water and earth elements as they negate the energy of the fire element. Do not use clay pots, watery items or wavy shapes. Try to keep rocks and square shapes away as well.

For a door in the Southwest or Northeast direction the relevant fang shut element is earth. Now you've realized that you can't paint the door in any of the corresponding colors of earthy shades or in pink and red. But what you can do is decorate in another way. Get clay pots in the colors of red and orange and a doormat in square shape. Get creative with other shaped objects such as triangles and stars as well.

The water, wood and metal elements are to be kept away. Do not go for decoration with big plants or too much of green. Avoid putting wavy shapes and black or blue pots nearby.

A door in the West or Northwest direction is supported by the element of metal. Now this one is tricky when it comes to décor. You might compensate for not painting the door in the colors of metal, by just getting it in metallic finish. And if you are unable to do that as well, try decorating with metal items. Get metal pots and vases that can be placed in the doorway. Or place a doormat that is either round or square shaped.

The fire and water element work against metal. So keep all red and blue colors away. Do not opt for black either or shapes that signify any of the elements of fire and water.

Lastly, there is the door facing the north. This is surrounded by the Fang Shun element of water. You can go for water items and colors such as blue and black for decoration. A metallic finish would also be complimentary. Metal objects can also be used. If you are placing a doormat, choose a shape that is wavy or round.

Wood, fire and earth elements are negative for the energy of the water element. Hence, you should be avoiding clay pots and too much of green all around. Stay away from the colors of pink, red and purple as well. Shapes should not be rectangular or square. Also avoid putting too much stones or rocks in decorating.

All these ways can help with the creation of a strong, positive Fang Shun even if you can't repaint or paint your door according to the element colors and directions that complement each other.

Chapter 17: Main Entrance Feng Shui

The previous chapter talked about creating a good Fang Shun in the main entry and front door. Here we are going to talk about the entire main entrance. Now you may be wondering how that is different from what we have previously talked about. Here is what this is about.

A main entrance covers the front area of the house. A good Fang Shun here determines the kind of energy that will be circulated through all the different rooms and places in the house.

So how can you try and ensure a good, strong Feng Shui in the main entrance?

Here are a few ways to do that:

-Maintain a positive flow of energy in the main entry.

The chapter before has already talked about creating a good main entry Feng Shui and how you can build upon that.

-Your front door should be attracting good energy.

A strong Feng Shui front door is very important. And all the information on how to establish that is given in the previous chapter.

-Your main entry rug should be of a suitable Feng Shui design and color.

It is advisable that your rug in the main entry should be matching well with the décor. It should be inviting the positive energy to circulate within the house. If you have a certain Feng Shui element and you have decorated accordingly, try to get the rug to match it as well. This enhances the Feng Shui effect.

There are certain aspects to be kept in mind for that. For the best choice of main entry rug; focus on the shape, colors and design.

Gut instinct plays a very important part in design. Whether it is of a home or anywhere else, one must always go with the gut feeling. But that does not mean that the designing basics should be foregone completely. Try to incorporate a little of both and you will be able to come with a design that is both aesthetically pleasing and personally satisfying.

While looking at a space in the room, try to figure out what works best there. Focus on the visual appeal of a shape and how it would look in that particular space. Then find out the direction of where your front door is facing, and choose the shape that is appropriate for the element that accompanies the direction.

Here's an example, if the door is facing is west, then get a rug shaped in a circular or square shape, since the element that complements the direction of west is metal. Avoid shapes symbolize elements that clash with metal, such as fire.

The colors that you should opt for should also be according to Feng Shui elements and their energies. In door facing East or West, you have choices from the elements of earth, wood and metal. Choose the colors that go with the energy of the appropriate element. Also keep in mind that if you choose colors from an opposing element, it will not attract the positive Feng Shui energy. In case of metal, the opposite would be a fire or water element.

The design of the rug is the most critical aspect. It is a rug placed on the rug, in the main entry; not only you, but other family members, guests and friends coming in, will be stepping on this every time. So in order to invite and attract good energy, opt for a design that does not affect the flow when people step on the rug. For example, avoid names, symbols such as flowers and birds or any figures of people. It is not a good sign when people step on birds, names and human figures. It hampers the flow of energy and is definitely not a source of attraction for good Feng Shui.

The best idea would be to go for an abstract design with shapes that are symbolic of the element of Feng Shui. You can also choose designs of stones, and pathways or anything that represents a smooth, solid ground. This can be really good in regulating positive energy. A solid ground signifies a good foundation and the energy can have a really positive impact on that.

-Another thing to consider in a main entrance design is the bathroom placing. It is facing the front, main door, then that is not good for the energy. The bathroom will lead to all the energy flowing out and none being left within the house. Now this can be a complicated situation.

People who live in houses where bathrooms face the front doors, and they aim to maintain a good Feng Shui in their house, should not be hassled by this. There are measures you can take to ensure that the energy remains in the house and does not flow out. If you have read up on Feng Shui, you already have an idea that the bathroom and front door close together can lead to a negative Feng Shui as well.

To avoid such a situation, keep the bathroom door shut off. This is an important tip regarding every bathroom. The energy flows out, no matter where the bathroom is situated in the house. But when it comes to the front situation, this becomes absolutely imperative. The door should be closed always.

The bathroom is considered a tricky area when it comes to Feng Shui, hence maintaining a good Feng Shui in there is challenging. Try and focus the energy in the area and choose the right colors and aesthetics.

The energy in the main entry should be strong and very positive. This will help enhance the Chi and it won't flow that easily through the bathroom facing the front door. The quality of the Chi that comes in the house should be well and good. If it's maintained in the main entry then the chances of it going out become low.

If you are able to create a good focus point in the area close to the entry, it will direct the energy away from the bathroom. The located focal point will help disseminate and reflect the energy towards the other rooms and spaces in the home. Set up a decoration piece, or decorate a wall with vibrant colors and paintings to help incorporate the energy and guide it elsewhere.

Make sure that the bagua areas of the bathroom and main entry are strong. If the energy of the bagua is strengthened, the Feng Shui of the entire house becomes strong and fresh. It certainly takes more effort when there are tricky areas such as the bathroom and garage involved. But if you are able to do this successfully, then your whole house can benefit from the positive vibes and energy.

-The alignment of the front and back door is an important point to be considered. To establish a smooth flow of energy, that is balanced and strong, one must figure out how the front and back doors are aligned. A direct alignment of doors will have a negative impact on the energy flow. There will be little or no energy left in the house as it will enter from the front and flow out from the back, similar to the motion of a liquid.

To ensure that the energy is circulated within the house and nourishes it, try a few simple tips, there is little one do about the door alignment when the house has been constructed. Put in small tables and set up flowers with vases in the path of the energy, this will slow the flow and even direct it otherwise. Play with colors, contrast or match the energy of the two doors with or against each other. This will also help with the regulation.

Plants are important in Feng Shui and if you use them strategically, they can help redirect and reflect the energies. Try placing a tall plant in a big pot in between the doors and use it as a barrier in the energy path. An arrangement of the furniture or other objects can also help with the direction of energy. Use a solid grounding rug with a bright color and attract that energy. If you even rearrange furniture such as sofas and chairs in between, it will help restrict the energy flow and prevent it from flowing out. If you cannot figure anything out with these settings, then just experiment with the décor. Use colors and aesthetics that appeal to the eye and are a visual treat.

-The staircase facing the main door can pose as a problem in the path of the energy. It presents the same problem of letting the energy out too quickly. So you have to try and slow the energy down and circulate it in other directions. Get help from colors, art, plants and strategically placed furniture that can harbor the energy and prevent it from going out through the staircase.

-Mirror placement are critical in maintain a good Feng Shui. It is important that there is no large mirror facing the front door. That will reflect the energy outwards, and not retain it within the house.

All these points are just to help you make sure that the main entrance of your house is facilitating a smooth and harmonious flow of energy. This is integral in building up on a strong Feng Shui within the entire house. The main entrance is the area where the energy starts to flow in, and if you are able to incorporate it with positivity and strength right there, the energy in the whole house will carry those good vibes.

Chapter 18: Feng Shui For the Stairways, Wind Chimes for the Home and Using Wallet Feng Shui to Increase Household Finances

Feng Shui for the Stairways

Stairways play a significant role in allowing the chi to move up and down with ease. Sufficient attention should be placed in the location and the design of the stairways so that they will not hinder the flow of the energy inside the home. Stairways should always have sufficient backing. Open risers disrupt the flow of energy. What happens is that those who are staying on the second floor are not able to receive the flow of luck. If one's home or apartment is located on the second floor then this should be remedied by adding risers.

Stairs that terminate at the door lead to health problems associated with the head and the neck. This also causes problems for the head of the household. If the staircase ends at the front door, the door must keep a bright light. Alternatively, a crystal may be hung between the staircase and the main door. Or if bad luck ensues, one can hang a tiny mirror on the back of the door. This reflects the energy back up the stairways.

The stairs should never face a bedroom door because this will cause the occupants of the room to suffer from depression and it places them at risk for developing thyroid problems. Stairways that end at a door produce killing chi; if a mirror reflects the stairs, this doubles the poison arrows. The stairs should never be located above a bathroom either. Otherwise, it will lead to a drain of energy.

Perhaps the worst possible option for staircases is the spiral type. Note how it looks like a corkscrew boring into one's household. Staircases like these should never be placed in the center of the house or they will lead to a decrease in the household's finances. Instead, go for curved staircases. A staircase placed in the health area will create health problems.

Split staircases are best avoided. Scissor stairs are not very likely to attract success. They cause the family provider to experience financial losses. If this type of staircase is blocking the door, this can be remedied by blocking the view of the staircase. A long strand of ivy may also be wound around the handrails as a way to counter the negative effects. Artificial ivy may be used.

Situate the stairs at the side of the home instead of placing them at the center or they will create a gap between the members of the family. Red carpets must be avoided. Note how they look like blood spilling down the stairs. To allow the increase of growing energy, choose wood or tile coverings for the stairs. Staircases that point towards a window cause the household and its occupants to lose energy. Correct this by installing shutters.

Refrain from placing water sources beneath the stairs. This includes ponds, aquariums and fountains. These can bring danger to one's children. Instead, use moneyboxes or wealth vases to be placed on the empty space beneath the stairs.

Wind Chimes for the Home

Wind chimes are among the most popular Feng Shui home remedies. One of the purposes of wind chimes is to lift the chi from a disturbed area. Another is to suppress negative energy. Wind chimes also invite help and good news to the home. Every homeowner should know how to use wind chimes to their full advantage.

Wind chimes are made from various materials. Wind chimes made from metal are best hanged in the northern, western and northwestern areas of the home. Meanwhile ceramic or glass chimes should be placed in the northeastern and southwestern directions. Place wooden or bamboo wind chimes in the eastern, southeastern or southern area of the house.

When choosing between solid rods and full rods, remember that they are equally effective. But if one's goal is to increase the energy in a specific room, then wind chimes with hollow rods must be used. On the other hand, if a person is attempting to tone down the chi, then wind chimes with solid rods may be chosen instead.

If there are three or more doors in a straight line, hang a wind chime in that area. To increase energy, use pagoda-shaped hollow-rod wind chimes. Avoid hanging wind chimes in such a way that the door or the people entering and leaving keeps hitting it. Wind chimes made from metal must never be placed on trees because it causes the metal and wood elements to clash. Lastly, don't place a wind chime directly over a spot where people rest or perform activities such as eating or working.

Using Wallet Feng Shui to Increase Household Finances

A provider and a homemaker are naturally concerned about the family's finances. Coupled with hard work and careful spending and saving, Wallet Feng Shui can be a way to attract wealth and multiply the financial resources of the household.

One thing to keep in mind is that the wallet must always be kept organized. Just like in room Feng Shui, clearing the wallet space helps get rid of stagnant energy hence, facilitating the flow of fresh and positive energy. The person in charge of handling the household budget should rid the wallet of things that do not represent or attract fortune. For instance, credit card bills and receipts or anything that may symbolize debt must be removed from the wallet. Likewise, garbage such as candy wrappers should not be kept inside the purse.

Some people have a habit of carrying around identification cards bearing their old names or maiden names. They must also be removed from the wallet. The same rule applies to cards that are no longer useful such as expired membership cards and old hotel card keys. Instead, keep the wallet filled with money because it symbolizes abundance. In short, the keeper of the household budget should make sure that the wallet's space is occupied only with essential items.

Another important thing to remember is to store one's wallet properly. The better care a breadwinner provides to his wallet, the better care the wallet will provide to his family. Remember that tossing the wallet anywhere is disrespectful and should therefore be avoided. Refrain from placing it on the floor. Avoid dropping the wallet particularly on the toilet floor. Instead, select a special area in the home to keep the wallet. One should keep it alongside other valuable possessions as a sign that the wallet is being treasured. If the wallet feels appreciated, only then will it attract more fortune for one's family.

To maximize the household's fortune, one should choose the color of the wallet wisely. As mentioned earlier, every color symbolizes a particular element, and each hue holds a special meaning. When it comes to wallets, black is a popular choice of color for both men and women. Perhaps this is because people instinctively sense that the color itself attracts wealth. As mentioned, the element associated with this color is water. This means that it will invite the money to flow in. If one's family's main source of livelihood is from a business, then black wallets are recommended. Patriarch and matriarch providers who rely on their careers to sustain the family should also consider using black-colored purses to attract more success in their jobs.

Heads of families should remember that when choosing wallets or checkbooks, one should try to stay away from the color red. Otherwise, it will burn away the family's fortune. As mentioned previously, this particular color represents fire. A brown wallet is recommended for people who are struggling with savings. If one or one's partner is having difficulty in keeping the household expenditure to a minimum, choose this earth color to help tone down spending habits.

While pink wallets may be good for single ladies who are trying to attract love and luck in relationships, family breadwinners should keep away from this color because like red, it will burn away one's fortune. Yellow money holders are also good for attracting wealth. However, go for the ones with a pastel or mustard hue. Light yellow shades tend to attract wealth but only briefly. Often, the money flows out as quickly as it flows in.

While one might think that making use of secondhand purses can help save more money for the family, the opposite is true. The energy of the previous owner can affect that of the present owner. There is a chance that one might end up with a wallet filled with negative energy. If this turns out to be the case, think of its damaging implications to the household. Of course, there's also a chance that one might get a lucky money keeper. However, owing to the fact that the previous owner has discarded it, chances are the wallet didn't bring them much luck. Hence, using a brand new container to hold the family's money is the soundest choice.

Wherever a person keeps the wallet, he should place three ancient coins and a red tassel next to it. This helps pull in wealth. The wallet's shape also creates a huge impact on one's funds. It is best to stick with long and straight wallets and check holders than irregularly shaped purses. Lastly, remember that one can tell a lot about a person in the way that he arranges money in the wallet. Individuals who simply stuff notes in their purses in a disorganized manner are at risk for losing their money. Keeping money in this way results in negative energy relationships between the person, the wallet and the money. Show respect and appreciation for money by placing currencies in an orderly manner and sorting them out in various compartments.

Chapter 19: Feng Shui Tips

This chapter is essentially a very important chapter! You will learn how you can ensure that there is a sense of calm in your house. This can be done through certain methods that do not take up too much of your time. Let us see how you can ensure that you have a good amount of positive energy in your home.

Seating, Shapes and the Spatial Relations

The energy in your house flows from corner to corner. If there is any obstruction in the flow of the energy, the energy may stagnate in that area. The arrangement of your seating and your beds play an important role in the flow of the energy. This section of the chapter covers the important aspects of this spatial arrangement.

The Sofa

The sofa or the couch is the one place you and your family sit in when you are spending time in the living room. This sofa needs to be placed against the wall. You have to make sure that your sofa is not blocking the main door since that is where the positive energy enters your house. You can always ensure that you have a view of your front door when you on the sofa. When you are placing the sofa, make sure you leave a little space between the wall and the sofa. This will ensure that the energy flows through the minute crevices found between the wall and the sofa.

If you have no walls in your living room, you can always use lampshades and other stereo items. You may be wondering how this can be done. Place the lampshades or the console on either side of the sofa. This leaves you with a feeling of security.

The Seating

The seating in your living room is of great importance. When you have people over at home, you want them to feel invited and calm. You could use the same seating arrangement on your porch and even in your bedroom. When you place the chairs in these areas, ensure that there is a good amount of gap. You do not want your guests to feel cramped when they are sitting in your living room. But ensure that the chairs are not so far apart that the people find it difficult to talk to one another. If the chairs have been pushed, as far back to the wall as possible, they would not be conversing with each other since this requires a certain amount of shouting. It is always a good option to have an arrangement that promotes an intimate conversation. This will invite people to converse with one another.

When you enter a restaurant or a coffee shop, you will look for a place where you can have a good conversation with the person you have entered the place with. You will always look for a place that has a wall to your back. This is because you are skeptical of having your back exposed. You find it safer to have the people you are talking to in front of you. This is why it is always good to ensure that your guests find seats at your home that make them feel comfortable.

The Tables

The tables may seem a very minute detail to you but they play a major role in the flow of energy in your house. You will have to ensure that you do not have tables that do not let people have conversations at. You may also want to have tables in your bedroom. You can go right ahead and do it, but it is best if you follow the rules that have been mentioned in this section. A rectangular table is a big no – no. This is because it has very sharp edges that do not let people walk around the table comfortably. People will need to be conscious of the way they are walking since they would want to avoid getting hurt. It is always good to have a table that is circular in shape. The same rule goes for your bedroom. If you have tables with pointy edges, you may walk into it and stub your toe pretty badly.

Windows, the Colors and the organized Clutter

This section is an extremely important aspect that you will need to keep in mind.

The Windows

The windows in your house play a major role in the flow of positive energy through your home. Let us assume that you have a large window that is right next to the main entrance. This will ensure that all the energy flows right out of your house. So what must you do to ensure that the energy stays in? You will need to place an obstruction. Have a curtain that is bright colored, hung on the window. When you find yourself feeling tired and dull, you can draw the curtains. There may be people who would love staring into your house. Ensure that you do not let them! If you find that they are invading your privacy, try to use curtains that are dark.

The windows in your room can be looked at in the same manner. You have to have windows that are east facing. If you do not have them, it is all right. But ensure that you have a certain amount of sunlight entering your home. It is always a good idea to wake up with the rising sun. This leaves you with a great amount of energy.

There may be times when you have a window that overlooks the drain system of the next house. You would never like to look at such a thing when you want to stare out of your window. You could instead decorate the window to ensure that there is a semblance of beauty to your window.

The Clutter

Clutter is a term that you had come across earlier. It is highly essential to get rid of the clutter that you have at home. You need to declutter your home in order to ensure that you have a good flow of energy. When you begin to declutter, you will find items that you never knew even existed in your home. This may remind you of s scene from the book 'Shopaholic takes Manhattan'. In this book, the protagonist, Rebecca Bloomwood goes into frenzy when she finds the different stores in New York. She buys all the items she comes across without giving it a second thought. She finds herself in immense debt when she gets back home. Her friend Suze then tells her that she must declutter! She must get rid of every item she never uses. She takes the challenge up but finds it difficult to part with the items that she owns. She takes air filled bags and stuffs them with the clothes and her other belongings and stuffs them into a different shelf. When Suze comes back, she finds that the room is clean! They find a table that has a purple top to it! They had never known that it existed. The same could happen to you! You may be surprised by the stuff you own! You may find many objects that you thought you never had! There could be pictures that you could use to improve the conditions of your house. You can use all the clutter to decorate your house! You must do this only if you are certain that the clutter does not have to be thrown away!

You may now wonder what the point of decluttering is. You have to remember that you are working on using all the things you have. You do not want to store things for the sake of it. When you find things you love, you can add them to your bookshelf and start writing your story. When you find something new, add that to the story line. Do not pile your items up. Begin using them!

The color

The color of your house is a very important aspect that you have to consider. When you have bright colors in your house, you will be able to spread a lot of energy. You will find yourself energized every morning when you wake up in a room that is bright red or blue! Avoid dull colors like the plague. You will find yourself feeling dull and lethargic when you are around such colors.

Décor

The décor plays a major role in the Feng Shui in your house. You will need to remember that you have to find the perfect furniture and decorative items that will match you and your house. The dining room and the kitchen are the most important places to have the best décor. This is because of the fact that you obtain nutrition from these places. The bedroom and the living room are important too since you will be able to work on your relationships only in these two rooms.

Feng Shui for Beginners: A Complete Guide to Using Feng Shui to Achieve Balance, Harmony, Health and Prosperity in Your Home and Life! – 3ʳᵈ Edition

Let us first talk about your dining room. You have to ensure that the décor in the dining room must be formal. It should represent who you are. It should reflect you and your family as a whole. The décor in your room can be made of wood. This will keep you grounded since wood represents the earth elements. Try having a round table in the dining area as mentioned above. But a rectangular table would not be a bad idea either. You would not have people sitting at the corner of your table! But if you find that a round table fits your room perfectly, go for it! You can have a carpet in the room since it helps in providing a very intimate atmosphere.

When it comes to the kitchen, you will need to have décor that connects you to the earth. You can have wooden cupboards and stone counter tops. Have a few plants in your kitchen too! If you have these already, you will have to work on keeping them clean. Make sure that your countertops are clean. Make sure that the plants in your kitchen are not dead either.

You have learnt the different ways you can use Feng Shui in your house to ensure that there is a good flow of energy in your house. The next two chapters deal with the benefits of Feng Shui. There are certain secrets that have been mentioned which will ensure that you have a house that is balanced with different types of energies.

Chapter 20: The Benefits of Feng Shui

The advantages of Feng Shui fascinate many people. There are multiple reasons for this fascination. For beginners, the art of Feng Shui may seem like a superstition. They may find it difficult to believe that the arrangement of furniture in their house can benefit them. But as they come to understand the depth of Feng Shui, they will be able to learn how the positive energy flows in their immediate environment through a change in the arrangement of the objects. But this is where the definition or the understanding of Feng Shui gets complicated. You may wonder how the arrangement determines the flow of the energy. There are many schools in different cultures that use Feng Shui as a method of housing.

The greatest part about Feng Shui is that any person can understand it easily. You do not need to have a degree to use the different methods of Feng Shui in your house. You do not have to spend too much money either. There are other advantages that make Feng Shui great. This chapter covers these advantages in detail.

Psychological Benefits

When you have the idea of coming back home from work, you have to find all the stress driving away from you. You have to make sure that your mind and your body will have a sense of relief. You need to feel lighter, content and more energetic. If you find yourself not feeling this way, you will have to work on it! You should not come home feeling irritated or restless or even overwhelmed. You should come back with a feeling of optimism. This can only happen when you embrace Feng Shui. Your body and mind will experience a sense of stability within which will have a positive effect on your family all through Feng Shui.

Environmental Benefits

You may wonder how arranging the furniture in your house benefits the environment. When you decide to add a plant to your house, you are adding an element of the earth to your house. This helps in grounding you and stabilizing your life. This balance is what helps in promoting the physical and mental growth of you and your entire family. There are different species that work on purifying the air. These species are a part of the earth and will ensure that your house is free of toxins. There was a research conducted by NASA, which concluded that human beings are subjected to different types of pollutants, mainly the indoor pollutants. The only way by which you can avoid these indoor pollutants is by adding flora and fauna to your house. These air-purifying plant species are Dwarf date palm (Phoenix roebelenii), Areca palm (Dypsis lutescens),

Kimberly queen fern (Nephrolepis obliterata), Variegated snake plant, mother-in-law's tongue (Sansevieria trifasciata 'Laurentii'), Red-edged dracaena (Dracaena marginata) etc.

Stability in life

When you find yourself stressed or under pressure because of the clutter you have at home, you will love Feng Shui. You will find that you are able to incorporate materials that are good for you through Feng Shui. You may have issues with what you see in front of you. Through Feng Shui, you will be able to ensure that there are objects that bring calm to your eyes in your home and in your immediate environment. You can have a garden out front with a lot of flowers and vegetables. This will leave you with a sense of grounding! When you begin to achieve stability through the minute things like the arrangement of furniture, you will find yourself achieving a greater sense of stability in the most important aspects of your life.

Mindfulness

You will begin to be aware of different things in your life. This is a very good thing since you will know what is happening with you and with the people in your immediate environment. Every human being makes the mistake of paying attention to the bigger picture and they forget what about the tiny memories, which make you who you are. This is called the art of living. The minute details that you will have to pay attention to are the way you arrange your home and the way you maintain that arrangement. If you ignore these ideas, you will only be building an environment that is stressful and will lead to many other problems in life.

The Feng Shui community

Feng Shui is a path on which you meet different people who are as enthusiastic as you. Some of these people may be experts. You will be able to meet many new people and will be able to communicate with them on a regular basis. You will be able to share what you experience through Feng Shui once you stop thinking of this as a silly culture or a superstition. There are chances in the Feng Shui community, you will end up finding another member within your network who has a similar taste like you and help you with any Feng Shui developments, no matter how insignificant.

A fresh new perspective

When you find yourself with a new perspective, you feel fresh and bright when compared to your old self. This perspective has to be a positive one since the negative perceptions bring you down. When you have a positive perception, you will find that you are able to invite changes into your life. Feng Shui provides you with a fresh new perspective of how you can design and arrange your home. This arrangement benefits you in the near and the later future. The benefits of Feng Shui contribute to the enrichment of one's mind.

Prosperity and Success

You would have learnt in the principles that Feng Shui helps in making you prosperous. Most people have adopted Feng Shui because of the fact that they want to become prosperous in life. You will find success with ease since you are both balanced and prosperous.

Aesthetic appeal

As mentioned in the principles of Feng Shui, you should remember that Feng Shui works on the symmetrical balance of all your objects. Since all the objects are symmetrically arranged, you will find that your home is beautiful. This symmetry gives your house an aesthetic appeal to both your house and your immediate environment. There is also a great physical appeal to a house that has been decorated using the principles of Feng Shui. It could also have a mental appeal to it through the positive flow of energy throughout your house. Feng Shui helps in promoting beauty in both the mental and physical forms of life. Feng Shui promotes beauty in both physical and mental forms of life.

The Twenty Simplest Benefits of Feng Shui

You have learnt about the different ways you benefit if you follow Feng Shui. Those benefits are on a large scale. This section talks about the benefits that would make you want to follow the path of Feng Shui!

- You will find yourself with a promotion letter or a hike in your salary
- Your health will drastically improve
- If you are looking to get married, you will find your partner with ease.
- Pregnancy becomes easier for you. You will also be able to avoid any miscarriages
- You may have problems with your partner but you will be able to sort them out before either of you takes any hasty decisions
- You will find yourself motivated at every step of the way
- You will find that there is harmony in your family and even at work
- If you are struggling to work on a project, you will find yourself with a renewed sense of concentration
- You will find that your creativity has no limits
- You will be more in control of yourself
- You will be immensely controlled in your office and your house. You will find that you are able to avoid any kind of imbalances in the way you feel
- You will find that you are never depressed in life

Feng Shui for Beginners: A Complete Guide to Using Feng Shui to Achieve Balance, Harmony, Health and Prosperity in Your Home and Life! – 3rd Edition

- You will have a social life that is buzzing with vibrancy
- If you own your own business, you will find that is has begun to flourish like never before
- You will find yourself safe from any issues on the legal front. You will also find that you are able to avoid the influence of any malicious person
- You will find yourself safe from accidents of any kind
- If you require new areas for shelter, you will be able to find them with ease
- You will be able to ward off any addictions
- You will find that you do not suffer from insomnia
- Respect and fame will find their way to you

Your life may be right on track. You may not have the need to work around your life. But there is no harm in practicing Feng Shui. You may be able to find yourself on this path. You will also be able to benefit by following this path. If you have mastered the art of Feng Shui, you could go and help your friends! You can always have fun with Feng Shui!

Chapter 21: The Secret Ways To Improve Your Feng Shui

There are certain secret tips that you can use to ensure that your house has a good flow of energy in it. These tips will help you ensure that you are sticking to the principles of Feng Shui. These are the Ten Commandments or the eight-fold path of Feng Shui. You will need to follow them word for word to ensure that you improve on your Feng Shui.

Find ways to add beauty to your home or workplace

This is an extremely important secret that you will need to keep in mind. Assume that your house has a lot of objects that you do not find to your liking. This will make you irritable and will make you feel distant from your home. It is always best to have objects and colors that beautify your workplace or your house to your interests and liking. This makes you happier and you will willingly do what you are asked to do at home or at work.

You can use different books on home décor and also on your workplace décor. There are many experts who have provided you with different techniques that you could use. For instance, you may have pictures of your family. These pictures may bring a smile onto your face. Hang them up on the walls at home and place a few on the desk at work. Bright colors bring a level of vibrancy in your house. You can use these colors to paint your walls. There are different types of furniture that you could use too! You can have different pieces of art that you may have collected on your many trips across the world. Try to showcase them! Decorate your living room with these pieces.

Remove the negative energy from your environment

You have to strive to remove even the slightest bit of negative energy from around you. The negative energy is not good for you considering the fact that it begins to overshadow the positive energy that is found in your immediate environment and in you.

You may have objects in your home that remind you of certain negative things. You will have to get rid of them this very minute! These objects could be anything from a letter to a picture of someone. There may be people in your life that you are close to. But it is these people who hurt you beyond anything you would have felt before. Instead of dwelling on such people, you can try to stay away from them. This will ensure that they do not suck on your energy and feed off of you to remain happy.

This holds true at your workplace too! You may have a job where the office is quiet and organized. You know that you can work there but there are certain things and certain people who make it impossible for you to work. There are times when you have a job that you dislike with all your heart. Do not work in such conditions. Tell yourself that you need to find something better than what you have now and that you deserve it. You can try to be like Rebecca Bloomwood. She worked as a finance expert and then got herself into an immense amount of debt. She believes that her life is over at the age of twenty-six. It is her friend Michael who pushes her to think otherwise. He offers her a fresh start. But she does not take that job up! She becomes a personal shopper in the United States. She chose to do what she loved and she flourished. You may find it terribly difficult to get out of what you have been doing so far, but think about this – will you be able to work in the same conditions for the rest for your life?

Identify, segregate and remove clutter!

This is a secret that you will need to follow word for word. In the series, 'The Shopaholic', Rebecca Bloomwood shops her way into debt. She feels that she needs to buy a certain item if it is on sale. She walks into a store and will only leave it when she has bought too much. She does not stop to think about whether or not she needs it. She jumps up at the opportunity to buy clothes or shoes or even a bag! This is something you need to avoid strictly. You have to ensure that you only buy the items that you require. You should not buy things that you THINK you require. You have to first sort your clutter and separate the things you do not require and the things you do require. You will be able to work on Feng Shui only then.

You should try to do the same when you go shopping as well. Only buy those items that you need. Make a list for yourself and ensure that you stick to that list! Only when you stick to the list will you be able to ensure that you do not have clutter at home.

Strike a balance between the energies in the environment

You need to strive to achieve a balance between the energies that you find in your immediate environment. You need to have the same or similar amount of both positive and negative energies. If you find that there is an imbalance, you must ensure that you change the look of your house or the way your objects are arranged. There are times when you may find yourself with an imbalance of energy due to the wrong positioning of windows.

Align yourself in good directions

It is very important that you align yourself to the best directions in the house. There are certain beliefs in the Chinese culture that a bed must never have the pillows facing the south. It is always good to have your head facing the east or the west. The best place is the east since you will be able to ensure that you are waking up with the sun! When you place your head in this direction, you will be able to ward off any bad dreams and may be able to cure insomnia.

You will also need to ensure that you arrange the furniture in your living room in accordance with the theories of Feng Shui. You will need to align all the furniture in your living room along the lines of good energy. You will need to be as picky as Sheldon Cooper. You have to ensure that you have a place that benefits you the best. He ensures that he is able to watch the television and talk to his friends at the same time. He also mentions the draft of wind. This is what you have to make sure you have in your position. This can be done even at work.

Avoid sitting under beams

You have to always avoid sitting under beams. You should ensure that you are nowhere near the beams. Lying down under them is a big no – no. When there is energy flowing in the room, the beams exert certain pressure on it. This pressure is exerted downward. If you have sat under a beam, you may have complained about the fact that your head feels heavy. This happens due to the pressure. There are times when you may have felt the heaviness but never realized that it was because you were under a beam. This is essentially the only reason behind the heaviness. If you want to avoid the heaviness, try to avoid being in the vicinity of the beams in your house.

Remove broken items on sight

When you find any objects that are broken, remove them immediately. You do not want the positive energy to manifest itself in these broken objects. The energy seeps through the cracks and will disappear. Make sure that you get rid of the broken objects immediately or at least fix them immediately. You do not want to attract the negative energy that comes with the broken items at home.

Never sit near a corner or a sharp angle

Let us assume that you have a study in your home where you are sitting on a table. If this table is pointing to a corner or is pointing towards an angled door or wall, you need to move the table away immediately. This is because of the fact that you attract negative energy whenever you sit near a sharp edge. This negative energy affects your health and your relationships.

It is true that in Feng Shui, square and rectangular shapes are preferred. The reasons are mentioned below:

1. It has been seen that people relate to these shapes in a better way. You could try to have an irregular shaped wall or a couch in your room if you want, but you may not be comfortable with it. Any angle less than 90 degrees is not found to be comforting.

2. You could have irregular shapes in your room. There are times when you may have noticed that you are very tired even when you have rested well. This is because there is no good chi in your room.

Try to make sure that you have a comfortable view of your house!

Try to make sure that you do not have a very strong flow of the chi

You cannot see the Chi; it is a known fact that the chi flows around you in the air and in the water around you. This is why the name Feng Shui has come which directly translates into wind and water.

1. You should try to avoid sitting next to a vent or sleeping underneath it.
2. You should avoid sitting next to open windows since the wind brings in the chi.
3. Your room may be at the end of the corridor and opening right into the corridor. You will need to create subtle obstacles to ensure that there is no harsh flow of the chi.
4. There are houses that are at the end of the street and open right into the street. The owners are often asked to plant shrubs or trees to ensure that the chi flows through their house gently.

You have to always ensure that the chi flows through in a very soothing manner. Try to have shrubs around your house if you have a lot of windows!

Try to have objects depicting water in auspicious areas

Water is the element that brings prosperity. If you have noticed, the houses near the beach or the river are more expensive when compared to houses in the city. This is why water is always associated with money. You should try to add elements of water in the East and the South parts of your house. You could have a miniature fountain or a pane with water running through it. You could have the object that Joey Tribbiani from the TV series Friends buys for his house!

You could also have an aquarium! The most important thing to do is to ensure that the water is clean. You have to also ensure that you have a very good flow! If you let the water stagnate, you are letting yourself create negative energy.

Always involve yourself with the process of Feng Shui

This is the final tip in this book. When you are working on Feng Shui, you have to try to ensure that you involve yourself further. This would mean that you must join groups and communities that work towards ensuring that their house is organized using Feng Shui. You will find yourself obtaining better ideas through this method. Through these different ideas you will be able to ensure that there is a good amount of positive energy that is flowing through the house. You will be able to enhance your way of life through Feng Shui.

Chapter 22: Myths About Feng Shui

As is the case with anything that is popular and appealing, it is same with Feng Shui. Whenever a lot of people will start practicing something or follow a trend, they will talk about it and share information. Not all of this information may be true, just like a rumor, it will spread around and there might not be any credibility to it.

With Feng Shui also there are a few common myths or even stereotypes that people typically associate with this.

So how do you differentiate between truth and myth?

Read about it, get information verified from credible sources or seek help of a practitioner and expert.

To make it easy for you, here are a few common myths that have been discussed:

-A red color front is lucky.

This is not always the case; since front door colors are relevant to their direction and element. A red color front door will only be lucky and encourage good Feng Shui if it is associated with the element of fire.

Do not assume that it is a general thing and just paint your door red. Find out the direction and follow the element.

-There are myths regarding water and plants indoors. People believe that having a bamboo plant or small fountain of water indoors is lucky for the house and helps with a strong Feng Shui.

Yes, they might be very useful and efficient for a good Feng Shui, but it makes no difference if you are unable to accommodate either of these in the house. It takes more than plants and water to create and arrange a room or space that builds up on the Feng Shui and strengthens it.

-It is generally believed by most people that flowers in the bedroom give bad vibes and accounts for a bad Feng Shui.

No, that is not the case. Flowers are something that actually enhances effects of Feng Shui, and having some placed in you room will only project good vibes. They carry amazing Chi and can have a good impact on the Feng Shui in the bedroom. However, keep in mind, that you must not overdo it. Place a small bouquet near the bed or keep a handful of flowers in a vase anywhere you like, just don't go for a too flowery or colorful decoration.

-Movement of furniture can have life altering impact.

This is also very much a myth. Moving a chair, sofa or table can only enhance the flow of the energy and guide it properly. There can be no life changing effects that can be produced from re arranging.

Do not expect to fall in love, get a job or something along the lines, when you change the arrangement in your house. For Feng Shui to work effectively, you have to combine a number of other factors together as well.

-There is a popular misconception that the direction of the bed can affect your luck and change your fortune.

No, that is absolutely not the case. The direction of the bed can have no affect whatsoever on your luck, relationship with your partner or influence any other aspect of your life.

-Money plants in Feng Shui can bring in money and help you with financial luck.

Sorry to say that this is not true either. There are significant types of money plants in Feng Shui, and you can find out information related to that. There is a money tree that is of importance in Feng Shui plants, but it is also not related to money and luck. Yes, there is a positive energy about the plants, and it nourishes the Feng Shui as well.

All plants are important in Feng Shui. They are symbolic of nature, the creator of energy. Hence, it is very useful for energy flow and nurturing if you have lush, green plants around your house. Take care of them as they can prove to be a healthy energy source and maintain its smooth flow. They can also bring you closer to nature.

Instead of wasting your time and energy in finding the right Feng Shui money plant, focus on the plants you already have and preserve their Chi within your house.

-The stove can help with a strong Feng Shui kitchen.

People commonly misperceive that the direction of the stove in the kitchen is relevant to the Feng Shui there. That is not the case. There are many other factors that can contribute to a good Feng Shui kitchen, and stove direction is not really of any importance.

If you are a person food of cooking and entertaining, focus on the wide array of elements that can account for efficient functioning in the kitchen. Do not worry about stove direction, just try and maintain a healthy, appealing kitchen that reflects happiness and contentment.

-Mandarin ducks are a symbol of eternal love.

Feng Shui can be effective in one's love life as life. There are many symbols and objects in Feng Shui that can have a very positive affect on a person's love life. Mandarin ducks are not one of those.

Generally believed to be associated with everlasting love, mandarin ducks are very common. They are widely found among people in China and even Japan, where people tell stories of how they mate for life and are very closely attached to each other. If you do not like the idea of this, it is completely fine. Not many people can related the idea of eternal love with mandarin ducks.

You can choose happy paintings, photographs of people and images of other animals that are known to stay together, such as swans or turtledoves. Whatever you opt for, make sure that it projects good, potent energy and can help move the blocked or negative energy around you.

-Displaying clocks around your home is bad Feng Shui.

That is not entirely true either. The size of the clock matters and so does it placement. Time is of great value and clocks are a reminder of how it passes by. Just don't display huge gigantic clocks on the walls, especially in the bedroom. Get clocks that are smaller and not necessarily displayed on the walls. Place these clocks where you view the time easily, but avoid stocking too many of them everywhere.

-A bagua mirror brings good luck and acts as a protection.

This is also a misunderstood concept. A bagua mirror, no matter in what size and shape has no effect on luck and is definitely not a protective force. A bagua mirror, regardless of its concaveness or how convex it is, should never be installed inside a home. It should be put outside if you have discovered that the energy surrounding you home is Sha Chi.

Sha chi is a negative Feng Shui energy that is also described as being an attacking force. If this kind of energy is coming in from the front of your house, then you can use a bagua mirror to deflect it back.

A bagua mirror outside your house will surely attract attention. If you want to avoid that, then use other objects to protect your house from such negative energy.

All these myths of Feng Shui create a lot of misconceptions among people. Those who have believed or followed any of these are now aware that these are all myths and should be dispelled. Always verify your information before you start acting on it. The presence of strong Feng Shui can be established by creating a positive and smooth energy flow in your home. Not by focusing on small, specific aspects and spending your time and efforts on those.

Chapter 23: Bad Feng Shui

Feng Shui is all about positive energy and good vibes that affect your personality, life and home in a good way. It is known for bringing prosperity and contentment to a person's life. However, not all Feng Shui is good.

Yes, there are bad Feng Shui energies that can have a negative impact on your life and home.

There is Sha Chi and Si Chi. Sha Chi means an attacking energy, something that is killing. While Si Chi means low, declining energy.

Sha Chi
This negative energy can be present both inside and outside the house. Outside it can be generated by a natural force or man-made structure that points towards the door of the house. It can be directed towards the windows as well.

Inside the house, there is the T-Junction aspect that can affect the direction of Sha Chi. It is believed that the Feng Shui inside a T-Junction house is bad and preserves the negative Sha Chi. The attacking energy is directed inside other areas of the house, and has a negative impact on the people that live there.

Sha Chi is an energy that can even develop inside a space. This can be because of any sharp angle that points towards a room, bed, and even towards the body. This sends the bad energy directly aiming towards someone's personal space and sometimes even at that person.

These sharp angles are referred to as poison arrows. They are responsible for all the circulation and direction of the negative energy around the house.

How do you lessen its effect?

Try to stay as far away from such angles and objects that emit the energy towards you or your space. The proximity is important. The further away the element giving out Sha Chi is located, the less will be its effect.

Si Chi

This is a term used to describe a slow, dying energy. As evident by this, it can have a very negative effect on a person if they are exposed to it for long periods of time. It can lead to depression, sickness and conflict among people.

This kind of energy is usually associated with places that were built in areas were human tragedies or destruction had occurred. Inside a house or space, such energy is generated by elements that can cause 'geopathic stress'. Now you might have not heard of this term.

That is okay, it is a relatively new phenomenon used to explain the relationship between the energies of earth and the well being of the people. The word geopathic is a combination of the 'geo' and 'pathic', where geo means land or earth, and pathic means the ability to sense and perceive something. In Feng Shui, pathic is something very interesting. It signifies illness and cure, two opposing energies.

The earth has a lot of energies; some of them can be very positive and beneficial for the people while others can be harmful.

In the olden days, the Feng Shui practitioners and experts were able to detect bad energies of the earth and recommend areas to build on. They could advise people on where to settle down and where to avoid going.

If you pass through a place that has geopathic stress and do not stay there for a long period of time, then it can have little or no effect on you. However, if you are located in an area with geopathic stress, then that could be a problem.

You might be wondering why this is so important. This is because when it comes to bad Feng Shui energies, like Si Chi, an area with geopathic stress can create and facilitate such energy. Si Chi especially, thrives in such a place.

Some of the factors to consider in an area with geopathic stress are the fault lines, magnetic and water currents, and electromagnetic fields that surround it.

The negative energy from geopathic stress can have a direct effect on a person's health and can lead to diseases and illnesses. That is why it is important to consider this. You might question how this can be.

Well, here's an explanation. If your house is near or above a highway or water body flowing under or near it, this can impact your health significantly. Water current or a magnetic force is generated near such areas, and if your bedroom is located close by than it can circulate around it.

This may not result in any illness or such but it can lower the immune defenses of a body. The forces present inside the body become focused on maintaining a balance, and all the energy that can rejuvenate and regenerate a body's system is drained away.

The easy way to figure out if your house has geopathic stress is to go through building plans. If there are errors in construction, unevenness, fault lines beneath or water seepage, then you can know for sure that it is present. You can try and look for possible solutions to lessen and negate its effects.

Then there is a second way to detect this, focus on the kind of energy and emotions that surround you or your family. If there is conflict, bad vibes and just an overall low feeling, then you have geopathic stress in the house. Some health concerns may also present themselves. Try and get help from a professional to direct such negative energy out of the house.

Check for damp and gloomy places inside your house or leakages. Put in more lights and illuminate the dark areas, fix and repair the broken or leaking places. This will also help and lessen the effect of geopathic stress.

There are other solutions to neutralizing the effects of geopathic stress as well. One can deal with this by enhancing the earth energies in the house. Try and create a healthy environment in the house.

As said before it is important to figure out the kind of energy that is in your house. You need to know what is directing such energy towards the house or a particular room. It could be water currents or earth line, or even a combination of both. The influence of these energies can be cyclical and varying. For example, the intensity of current of water or electromagnetic field can determine the kind influence of the energy that will surround a particular space.

Even if you live in an apartment or on any top floor, the energy can be felt just as strongly. This is because of the building materials that are used.

To negate and neutralize the effects of geopathic stress, you can follow some of these very simple tips as well:

-Move your furniture around.

Repositioning a bed, chair or table in a room where you and your family spend a lot of time in, can redirect the energies elsewhere and away from there.

-Use tools that can helps with the harmful vibes of the energy.

You will be surprised with how many tools are available in the market that can combat the negative vibes of bad energy. Some these include harmonizers, pyramids and even crystals.

A simple and common method is placing copper or brass wires and rods in certain rooms and areas around the house. This can block the negative flow of energy and protect the space around it.

-Personal tools are also available for directing the energy from geopathic stress away from a person.

With the help of technology and various other elements, there are specific items and materials that are made for blocking and redirecting negative energy. You will find them in the category of Pendants (personal or tesla). They can look like a piece of attractive jewelry or just a simple material that can be worn anywhere. They can be made with silver, gold and crystals.

Do extensive research and figure out where and what kind of energy you want to deflect. Then resort to purchasing these items and tools.

Bad Feng Shui House Features

After so much information about negative energy created by external factors, let's go on to some factors that can create bad Feng Shui within the house.

If you are looking to buy or build a new house, here are some checks that you should run:

-Alignment of front and back door.

Make sure that the front and back door of your house is not directly aligned with each other.

-The staircase facing the front door.

This is also a factor in the circulation of bad Feng Shui, as this hampers the flow of energy.

-Bathroom and front door facing each other.

There is clash of energy if there is a bathroom directly facing the front door. And this cancels out the good energy that enters the house.

-A staircase is positioned in the center of the room.

This invites bad Feng Shui and is not advised, regardless of the type, color and material used in its construction. It creates disequilibrium in the energy force and disturbs harmony.

-Bathroom is situated in the center of the home.

The center of a house is considered its heart, and is also the point of yin and yang force. It is the area where all the other rooms and spaces get their energy circulation. Hence, it should be open, well decorated and visually pleasing.

A bathroom there will not have a positive effect on the energy of the house.

-The master bedroom over the garage.

Try to avoid situating the master bedroom over the garage. The garage has lots of activity and movement of energy that might clash with the energy in the bedroom and have an opposing effect on it.

It will lead to sleeping problems and restlessness.

-Narrow, long hallway can create bad Feng Shui.

This kind of a hallway can harbor the energies of Sha Chi and Si chi, both of them can have a negative impact on the lifestyle and well being of the people in the house.

You can avoid the negative energies by decorating smartly and creating good vibes in the area.

Signs of a good Feng Shui house

You already know now about the features that can lead to a bad Feng Shui in the house. If you want to know about the signs that signify a good Feng Shui in and outside a home, here are some aspects to look at:

-There is a good Feng Shui outside the house.

The exterior of the house determines a positive external force outside the house. Look at the kind of formation that a house stands upon, whether it is T-Junction or a sloping house.

This can affect the generation of energy that will enter the house and give positive vibes.

If there is a small garden or lots of greenery and plants surrounding the front of your house, it can have a very good effect on the energy.

-No obstructions in the way of the front door.

Clear the pathway to the front door. There should be no big pots, bins that block the flow the energy.

-The quality of energy in main entry is good.

You have already been given all the necessary information regarding the flow of good energy in the main entry. Apply those and build on the quality of energy here.

-There is a good Feng Shui trinity.

If there is a good Feng Shui in the three main centers of the kitchen, bedroom and bathrooms, then there will be a positive energy in the center as well. They are the three energy focal points in the house, hence known as trinity. If the energy harnessed in these areas is good, the overall effect on the house will be positive as well.

-Fresh and free-flowing Feng Shui.

The energy around the house is in constant circulation. Hence it is important that it is fresh and regulated freely around every room. Any old or blocked energy can create a clash and neutralize the energy effects. De-clutter regularly, clear and clean all spaces in the house, try maintaining open and airy design. This will lead to a good Feng Shui circulation and bring in fresh light and air.

If there are all such features in a house, then it has good Feng Shui.

They will help keep the bad Feng Shui out and help one benefit from positive and healthy energy circulation.

Chapter 24: Feng Shui for Protection

This chapter will share a few tips and ideas about Feng Shui regarding protection. There are certain cures in Feng Shui that can help protect a person and their house against bad energy and negative vibes.

If you are looking to protect your house against bad Feng Shui, here's what you can do:

-Start with a strong and solid front door.

-Try to ensure that your house has a solid 'back'.

Having a good backing is important. It accounts for strength and support. Decorate your backyard well, and try to retain the energy there. Set up a garden or big plants there, use tall lights and garden walls.

-Use your knowledge of Feng Shui to create a garden that helps in the circulation and creation of good Feng Shui. This will lead to a vigorous energy flow and can act as a protection wall around the house.

-If you bad energy coming in from your neighbors, protect your house with fences, garden walls and strategically placed objects to block negative energy. Try positioning reflective surfaces that can direct the energy away or back to where it came from. In the areas where the negative energy is particularly strong, use colors and elements to redirect it and neutralize it; try paintings, décor and certain objects that can diffuse such energy away.

-Tortoise is a Feng Shui cure. The tortoise is one of the signs of protection in Feng Shui, it can be used to strengthen the energy flow and maintain circulation.

Place it in the back of your house or even in the garden, and ensure a good vibe of energy.

-Cultivate happy energy. This is simple, having a happy uplifting vibe of energy in the house can protect against bad Feng Shui.

-The symbol of dragon. This is a traditional cure of Feng Shui, and is a symbol of strong male and yang energy. Place it in accordance with direction of energy and it will act as a protection and harness the energy of the bagua areas effectively.

-Stones and crystals have a lot of purposes in Feng Shui. They can be used for protection as well. Choose the right ones carefully and place them properly in house for maximum effect. Hematite and black tourmaline may be most effective when it comes to protection.

-Bagua mirror is also common with Feng Shui. It should be used carefully, figure out which one to get for protection and place it appropriately. It is not a décor item and should only be placed outside. Its purpose it to fend off bad energy; it should not be used as anything else.

-Wind Chimes. Tall wind chimes can be effectively used as a source of protection if appropriately placed in the right bagua area. It is more appropriate if you place it outside and not inside the house.

-Fu Dogs.

If you have been to a Chinese or any oriental place, you have seen the Fu dogs or guardian lions placed outside, near the entrance. They are usually placed in pairs and are known as a strong source of protection. Place them in the entrance and near the front door if you want to try this.

-The symbol of the elephant. This is related to wisdom, health and protection in Feng Shui. The elephant symbol is responsible for generating a strong and positive flow of energy in the home.

Place the elephant motifs or structure near the entrance of your home, and for a better protection, get them in a pair.

-Water is also quite helpful in directing the bad energy away and acts as a protection against it.

-The Buddha statue. This is a protective source.

If you are feeling adventurous and have the space for it, put in a statue of the Buddha there. This helps wards off bad vibes and ensures protection.

The statue and 'mudra' that is advised as being effective here, is the 'no fear' one.

-The right color of the front door can also be protective.

-One of the most common symbols in Feng Shui is the mystic knot sign. It is combination of the infinity symbol, integrated with each other six times. Find out how it can be efficiently used in protection and get the appropriate one to use as protection.

-Illuminate the house numbers outside. This will increase protection, as having a well-lit and bright number of the house can be a good sign for protection and attract a positive energy as well.

-Round or sphere shaped objects. You might have seen a lot of sphere shaped objects in many people's houses. They go well with modern design and are a protective symbol as well. It has a reflective surface as well and can help direct the negative energy away as well.

-The color red is associated with the element of fire. This increases its protective powers and wards off bad vibes.

-The dragon horse or Chi Lin is a mythical creature in Chinese mythology. It has the body of a horse, face of dragon and scales of a fish. It is known as a unicorn horse as well. It is associated with loyalty and prosperity, and can be a very efficient protective symbol as well.

It should be placed near the entrance or in the family living room, do not put it in any other room. You can get it embroidered somewhere or as a sculpture, and even carry it around in a key chain. In Chinese mythology, it is known to keep the evil eye and spirits away.

-Bead designs. The Dzi bead design is also a very powerful symbol. It is usually in the image of an eye. The eye is protective and watches out for bad spirits. If you get a design placed near the entrance of your house or near the door, it will act as a protection and watch out for negative energy.

-The symbol of yin yang. Most people believe that this promotes and harbors harmony and balance. They are right, it does. It can also be uses in house protection.

-Maintaining a strong center in your house can help with strengthening protection as well.

-The Pi Yao energy can also be harnessed for protection.

-A person's Chinese zodiac sign and using it in your home can also enhance the protective energy around the house.

These were some of the tips and information on how to harness the Feng Shui to strengthen protection and positive energy around and outside the house.

Chapter 25: The Simple Eight Point Guide To Life!

You have gone through the different ways you can Feng Shui up your house. You may be overwhelmed with the amount of information that has been given to you. But, there are certain things that you have to remember in order to ensure that you do not fail to comply with! These rules or tips comply with eight different aspects of your life!

Money

This component is an essential part of every human being's life! It is true that there are things you cannot do or achieve in life if you do not have money. To ensure that there is a good inflow of money, you could try to place a bouquet of jade flowers or fresh flowers in your living room! You can maybe hide your treasure in the soil of the plant too!

Reputation

Your reputation directly hits your prosperity or your fame! You will need to ensure that there is no bad energy in the fire region of your house! You could use your awards to decorate the place. You can have your medals hung up or have symbols that are associated with good luck, like the four – leaf clovers.

Relationships

The relationships that you share with the people around you are very important. You have to find a way to balance the Bagua area that deals with your relationships. You could have objects that have pairs in the room. You could have lovebirds or cranes or even butterflies. It is also good to have a pair of doves if you like. If your bedroom is in that area, you could have colors representing love or have a love pillow. If it is in your living room, you could have matching chairs.

Children and your creativity

You may have lots of children or no children at home. In the areas of your house that are associated with your creativity and your children, you could have colorful art put up. You could have a bulletin board or a lot of chart papers that you could use to enhance the creativity of your children. If there are no children at home, you could use this space to indulge your inner child! You could use paint or crayons to brighten up the place!

Friends and Travel

Your friends play a major role in your life. You always need a group of friends to stick by you no matter what it is you are going through. You will have to see if you have such people. In the area that is associated with friends, you could have funny pictures of all of you! You could do the same with travel! You could have funny pictures and a have a map that will remind you of the area that you travelled in. You will be able to identify the places that you visited during your travels!

Your career

You will only be able to obtain wealth and prosperity when you have a good career. You need to ensure that the area that is associated with your career has a good amount of energy. You can brighten the place up as well as you can! It may be possible that you have the area associated with your career as your living room or even the entrance. Try to brighten the place up using a chandelier. Since you know what it is that you want to do, you will need to make sure that the place associated with your career has certain objects that are associated with your career. For instance, if you are a painter, you could have brushes and paints and even the canvas in the area!

Knowledge

It has been specifically said that you need to ensure that the energy in the room with the fire element of the Bagua needs to be considered with great importance. This is because this element deals with your knowledge. You will need to have a good amount of knowledge to live in this competitive world. You could have a bookshelf or your reading couch. This area could also have a space to have an intimate conversation if you ever need to have one! You can also meditate in this place! This helps you balance the fire energy by the thunder!

Family and their health

Your family is the most important thing to you. Their health is even more important. The area that is directly associated with your health and that of your family's must be kept extremely clean you will need to ensure that you maintain this area well. You could have a photo board or a storyboard in the area!

Feng Shui for Beginners: A Complete Guide to Using Feng Shui to Achieve Balance, Harmony, Health and Prosperity in Your Home and Life! – 3rd Edition

Key Highlight

You know that Feng Shui is the best way to ensure that you have a good amount of positive energy flowing through your house. In the first chapter you learnt what Feng Shui is and also learnt about the history of Feng Shui. You came across the different instruments that are used for Feng Shui and also learnt about the modern practices of Feng Shui. You have also learnt how you to ensure that you have a good amount of energy can use the modern techniques.

The next chapter deals with the different theories of Feng Shui. There are three major theories that have been covered in detail. You have learnt that these theories are interrelated and play a major role in establishing a balance between the energies that exist in the house. The five elements theory and the Yin and Yang theory work on the principle that the universe is filled with energy called the Chi, which is found in every entity. There are different principles of the Feng Shui that have been mentioned in the chapter too! You have learnt that the principles used in Feng Shui are adequate and help you achieve a balance in your life.

You have then come across the modern Feng Shui theory of the Bagua. This is a mix of the five elements theory and the theory of the universal energy. It is the best theory that has been used till date. You will find that you have a good balance of energies in your house when you use this theory.

You then learnt about the steps to ensuring that your house has Feng Shui in in. The first step to Feng Shui is to declutter. But what is clutter? You learnt about the three types of clutter. You understood the reasons why the three types of clutter exist. You have then learnt about the seven-step process for decluttering. You can follow these steps to ensure that you have decluttered your house and made it ready for Feng Shui.

Once you finish decluttering, you will be able to ensure that you have enough objects and space to begin Feng Shui. You have enough space to begin arranging the different objects.

You then learnt about the different ways you can apply Feng Shui to the different rooms in your house. You can begin by concentrating on your bedroom and your living room since these are the places in which you build your relationships. You have then been provided with the knowledge of how to use the space in your house. You have also learnt how you can work with the different types of décor at home.

You then learnt about the different benefits of Feng Shui. There are different psychological benefits that will help you ensure that you have a balanced life. You learnt that you could ensure a certain amount of stability in life as well. The final chapter dealt with the secrets of Feng Shui. When you use these secrets and follow them word for word, you will be able to ensure that you have a balanced life forever!

Conclusion

Thank you again for purchasing this book! I hope this book was able to help you to understand how you can harness the power of Feng Shui to improve every aspect of your home and life.

The next step is to follow the suggestions here to start attracting balance, harmony, health and prosperity. It is only when you put your heart and soul into something will you be able to come out in flying colors. When you are skeptical about the journey you are undertaking, you will find it terribly difficult to complete the journey! You will need to constantly motivate yourself. If you think you work well as a team, you can incorporate your family into the process!

The penultimate chapter contains a few things that you will have to remember to ensure that you have a good flow of energy in your house. It is good to have a lot of chi, but you should ensure that you are never in the presence of a gust of chi! This is not very good. You have to remember that too much of something is not good at all! All the best with your new venture! I truly hope that you achieve prosperity through the methods that have been mentioned in the book.

Finally, if you enjoyed this book, please take the time to share your thoughts and post a review on Amazon. We do our best to reach out to readers and provide the best value we can. Your positive review will help us achieve that. It'd be greatly appreciated!

Thank you and good luck!

Made in the USA
Middletown, DE
15 August 2016